PRAISE
MAKE YOUR OWN LUCK

'Everyone works hard but not everyone gets lucky in life. This book shows us how to help tilt the odds of luck and success in our favour by doing the uncommon things'
—Sanjeev Bikhchandani, *Co-Founder, Naukri.com & Info Edge*

'A must-read for anyone wanting to be a better version of themselves and make things happen instead of cruising along in life. Good investment of time to learn from the experiences of the authors. What is called luck is often the result of consciously doing certain things'
—K. Ganesh, *Co-Founder, BigBasket, FreshMenu, HomeLane, TutorVista*

'I can relate to the lessons in this book—having lived them and seen them performed by successful founders I have backed'
—Anupam Mittal, *Founder, Shaadi.com*

'Successful salespeople always make their own luck. This excellent book shows you how to do that through unconventional ideas, strategies, stories, and specific instructions. If you want to grow your sales, get this book today!'
—John Henley, *CEO, The Center for Sales Strategy*

'Part inspirational and part instructive but fun and emotional at the same time—Rehan and Bob show you that luck comes to those who embrace it. Enjoyed reading how they got started like everyone but achieve what so many only dream of. A must-read for every soul who ever harboured an ambition'

—Nistha Tripathi, *Bestselling author of No Shortcuts*

'During the early days of angel investments, I would have the fastest finger to invest in a startup where Rehan was the lead investor. Happy to see Rehan unravelling some of the mystery behind his persona through this book *Make Your Own Luck*. The book shares many easy-to-learn insights to improve the odds of success. And also, great timing for the release of the book, as the Indian economy is getting enveloped by the startup ecosystem; and my sense is every startup entrepreneur will benefit from reading this book'

—Harish Mehta, *Co-Founder, NASSCOM*

MAKE YOUR OWN LUCK

How to Increase Your Odds of Success in Sales,
Startups, Corporate Career and Life

**BOB MIGLANI
REHAN YAR KHAN**

FiNGERPRINT!

Reprint 2024

FiNGERPRINT!

An imprint of Prakash Books India Pvt. Ltd

113/A, Darya Ganj,
New Delhi-110 002
Email: info@prakashbooks.com/sales@prakashbooks.com

Fingerprint Publishing
@FingerprintP
@fingerprintpublishingbooks
www.fingerprintpublishing.com

ISBN: 978 93 8917 845 6

This book is dedicated to those who are hungry to grow and have a desire to unleash the limitless potential within to make a positive contribution to their work, their families, and their life.

Luck lies not on the outside but within you. Let it out.

I believe in you!

-Bob Miglani

To the #Misfits, who were always told that their methods, ideas, and skills were insufficient, outlandish, abnormal and unacceptable. Those who had no choice but to take the hard path all through life, but never gave up.

-Rehan Yar Khan

ACKNOWLEDGEMENTS

I would first and foremost acknowledge my wife, Shefali, my kids, my parents, and my sisters, and brothers for their encouragement and kind support. Writing a book is really hard but your generosity and understanding gave me the room to create something that I hope will help make a positive contribution to improving someone's life.

I would also like to acknowledge our literary agent, Anuj Bahri for his friendship, mentorship and patience which helped guide us towards completion of this endeavour. Thank you. To our publisher and editor, Shikha Sabharwal and Vidya Sury. Thank you for believing in our message and helping us to share it with the world.

And of course, I would like to acknowledge my co-author Rehan Yar Khan who showed passionate curiosity, a keen intellect, and a desire to create something that withstands the test of a pressure cooker that is often the startup world. Through our vigorous and lengthy Skype calls over the past couple of years and our weekends talking for hours in NY and Mumbai, I learned a lot in this journey. Thank you.

Bob Miglani

I was never the one who got it right; in fact, I mostly got it wrong. I am blessed to be surrounded by many inspirational and supportive people my whole life, who have been my safety net and allowed me to get up when I was down.

My gratitude goes out to:

First of all, my parents who have supported me when I decided to become an entrepreneur in 1992. Thereafter, they continued to support me each time things didn't work out. They have been my backbone.

My friends, who have been as close as family. Always unquestioningly supporting and never judging.

My team members and partners, I could not have done it without you.

The people of the city of Mumbai, a welcoming ecosystem that supports entrepreneurs, and encouraged me with open arms every step of my journey.

Our literary agent Anuj Bahri, our publisher Shikha Sabharwal and editor Vidya Sury, for patiently working through our edits and rewrites.

My co-author Bob Miglani, whose idea it was to write this book in the first place; and who did most of the writing. Through his visits to Mumbai and numerous calls from New York, he carefully compiled my stories and insights and put them together into flowing prose. It has been great working with you, Bob.

Rehan Yar Khan

CONTENTS

INTRODUCTION

- Bob

"How did you make $75 million dollars for investors—from $100,000 dollars, Rehan? That is so incredible. Congratulations, man!"

This was my question to Rehan over dinner one evening in Mumbai some years ago. "I got lucky, Bob", he answered, with great humility. "I have been leading investments in a number of companies and some of them got very lucky."

We shared a smile and I thought, yes it was luck. But before beginning to enjoy our dinner, I became curious. A basic set of questions still nagged at me.

How could randomness favour this guy? Why *him*? Why not me? Why not so many others? Was there something about him that made him luckier than others? Or was he truly brilliant?

How could he possibly predict—with great accuracy—which investment, which idea or which founder was going to hit it big? How could he possibly be so right, so often? It wasn't just that one investment in Ola Cabs, where he led the first round. It was his startup, Flora2000. It was his work and investment in many startups. How did this guy get so lucky?

I could have easily dismissed his work in creating billions of dollars in value in multiple startups as a favour of the Gods or the universe and had a nice dinner with a friend—but I didn't. I followed my curiosity and asked Rehan more questions. And more. We talked for hours and again at breakfast another day.

As I started to peel back the layers of the seventy-five-million-dollar story, I began to understand the journey that led him from his failure in the floral seed import business to success in the telecom services business, then again, failure and later success in the international online floral delivery business. Then, onto leading angel investing as a means of helping founders realise their dreams and later, to setting up a venture capital fund to invest in startups.

Two things emerged that evening and later, over breakfast with Rehan, who is now one of the most successful investors in the world of startups.

The first was that luck, in Rehan's case, generating hundreds of millions of dollars from investing a few hundred thousand, came from a series of conscious choices and decisions. These often coincided with chance and random meetings with people who founded these companies, and whose valuations had unicorn status in the billions.

So, it was a series of choices. Not that he went to a good university. Not that he had the best grades in school.

Some of these choices were forced upon him while

others were proactive. Later, it was running into the right people—again by chance and randomness.

The second thing that emerged was the realisation that I too had followed very similar decisions and choices thrust upon me as a result of chance and randomness in my corporate career.

"You are lucky yourself, Bob. Having a successful and illustrious career at Pfizer for 23 long years is rare in today's corporate world. Your achievement of becoming a #1 sales rep for Pfizer, to later creating new divisions and opportunities in such a big organisation is remarkable," Rehan said to me at that dinner.

Hey, I'm not the one who generated the $75 million man, I first thought to myself with some disappointment. Or perhaps in envy of Rehan's financial success. But as I mused over it, I realised that yes, I am indeed a lucky guy. Growing up in Rampur, a village in India where we had nothing, then getting a chance to immigrate to the US and somehow landing in a company where I got to work on big ideas and create them into successful opportunities in one of the top companies in the world. Yes, luck did favour me in my corporate career.

After discussing our respective journeys, Rehan's in India with entrepreneurship and investing; and mine in the US in NYC with a corporate career in Pfizer Inc., one of the biggest and best companies in the world, writing books, and going from being a #1 salesperson to advising CEOs, we realised that we had plenty in common. Our being lucky had a lot to do with very similar choices we made—choices that looked like the right ones only later on in life.

What was amazing to me was that Rehan and I shared and believed in the same key principles and came to follow them instinctively. We learned the same lessons on our very diverse journeys to becoming successful. And those lessons were not the same old business lessons we were so tired of hearing:

"Work hard and you'll succeed."

"Do something you are passionate about"

"Find the right place, the right time"

Bullshit, we thought.

We all work hard. We are all passionate. But some of us are just not making it. Success is elusive. Why aren't more people becoming super successful?

The traditional approach to success of working hard and following your passion is simply not good enough for today's startup, sales, or corporate person who is trying to become lucky—to become super successful.

You might be asking, "Why? Why doesn't the traditional approach work anymore?" And that is largely because there is so much more competition in our job, career, startup world, and in life. There are more people in the world today who have strong work ethics and ideas for startups or a similar education or area of expertise. And so, in this new world, we must forge a new set of rules that will lead us to success.

No one was talking about the counter-intuitive approach to luck and success that we had learned in our journey.

And so, we came up with this idea of sharing our message with hard-working startup entrepreneurs, salespeople, and corporate climbers who were working hard but not getting anywhere.

We resolved to help others to learn from our failures and successes in a way that would jumpstart and boost their chances of success. We wanted to help these people who seemed to be doing everything right but weren't finding success as promised to them by the traditional model of success.

Thus, this book was born.

This book was born out of a desire to help you grow fast. Help entrepreneurs grow their business by 100x. Help corporate climbers elevate their careers to the sky. Help salespeople build super successful strategies. And many others achieve great success.

And we share it with you today to help give you an edge. Yes, you do have to work hard. But you also need to work smart. And being smart means making choices and decisions that will increase the odds of your success. Doing unconventional things that tilt the world of success in your favour.

With that, we say congratulations to you!

By picking up this book, you have increased your odds of success. By reading this book, you will improve your chances of success. By thoughtfully applying the principles laid out in this book, you will have effectively doubled your chances of success at achieving anything you want in life.

Whether you're building a startup, trying to grow your sales, or boost your career in a company, or pursuing a path of learning and growth in any field of endeavour, we believe that it is absolutely possible to radically enhance the level of your success to new heights.

For far too long many people have lost momentum in their lives—they've lost the motivation to pursue greatness because of the feeling that luck doesn't favour them. That for some reason beyond their earthly knowledge, the goddess of luck and chance has not blessed their path, no matter how hard they try. Others have felt that success was beyond their reach because they weren't born into the right family, have the right looks, or that they were not lucky enough to get the right job in the right company. Or that they did not have the same chances at success because they didn't go to the right school or university as other people.

But here's what we have realised: achieving remarkable success in life is not necessarily about being born lucky.

Breaking the Luck Myth - Rehan

You don't have to go to the right college.
You don't have to be born into the right family.
You don't have to have the best grades.

Achieving Success Comes from Making Your Own Luck

In my career as an entrepreneur who failed several times before finding success in my own startup, Flora2000, to then becoming a successful angel investor and currently a venture capitalist, I have learned something crucial. What we often assume as stumbling onto success by chance is, in fact, the unimagined result of the deliberate choices we make in life.

Yes, there are those who are either born lucky or run into luck through an unintended chance. But that not what happens to most of us. So, don't wait for it or count on it. Go get it.

You cannot wait to run into a founder of a startup who asks for your investment in the greatest idea worth billions. You have to prepare for it, work for it, get ready for it. Yes, I was the first person to lead the investment in Ola Cabs when no one else was willing, turning $100,000 investment into $75 million. Yes, I was the first investor in Druva, which is amongst the most successful software product company to come out of India. And yes, I have had much success—and failure—in other investments.

I didn't go to the best university. I didn't have the best grades or the highest academic rank. I wasn't born into a wealthy family. But I made choices and encountered chances that were unconventional. I didn't follow the usual path. I followed a different path.

But what steered me along that path of chance and luck was not a stumble onto a perfect business plan. It wasn't even a lucky meeting with the founders of these great startups. It is what Bob and I are calling "Luck Accelerators"—they led me on the path of success in Ola, Druva, PharmEasy, Country Delight and several others I have seen grow from small ideas into billion-dollar companies.

These seven luck accelerators are the secrets of success. When embraced and adopted wholeheartedly, they have the potential to bring you great rewards not only in the world of startups but also in leapfrogging your career ladder up the corporate world, such as the one travelled on by my friend and co-author, Bob Miglani.

Sales Success to Corporate Success – Bob

What is considered success in a corporate career? Is it holding a high position? Working at a large and successful company? Is it consistent growth through promotions year after year? Is it stellar sales performance? How about making good money with benefits and stock options? Or rapid rise and favour with senior management? What about getting to travel to 30+ countries? Doing work that you enjoy? Or does success in a corporate career mean longevity in an increasingly cutthroat culture where layoffs and downsizing is the new norm?

By all of these standards, I have been very lucky as I got to experience success in all of these areas. Going from being born poor in a village in India to serving cones in my family's ice-cream shop in New Jersey, to getting an excellent education provided by a loving family. This alone can be considered lucky. But I also got to achieve amazing success in my twenty-three-year corporate career at one of the biggest companies in the world—Pfizer Inc.

What I discovered from my career—becoming a #1 sales rep to creating new departments and new opportunities and strategies at the highest level in a large company—is that while some people might get lucky by being close to the CEO or being friendly with someone important, their "success" doesn't last very long.

True success in achieving strong sales performance or growth in an organisation relies on the same luck accelerators that Rehan has experienced. **It's about choices and chances.** The choices we make—each day, through the good times and bad—proactive choices that result in true long-term success and growth. These choices lead us towards discovering new ideas, new products, new services, new ways of reaching more customers. They help us become receptive and open to new ways of thinking and help push us forward through difficult problems, turning them into amazing opportunities. We choose to put in effort and contribution. We make choices that are within our control.

Success is about the chances we encounter and what we do about them—the chance meetings, running into someone randomly—and what we do to fully take advantage of them.

Like Rehan, I too wasn't born into a wealthy family and didn't attend the best college. In fact, I was born poor in a small village in U.P, India. But I too got lucky. I made the best of the chances I was given and made unique choices that led me on the path to success.

Many Different Paths – One Key to Success

If we want to be successful, our view of luck must change.

When we perceive it as something random that happens to us by chance, we end up waiting for it for most of our lives.

We believe that while some of us experience some lucky events in life through circumstances that are out of our control, most of us arrive at those pivotal events through the accelerated luck paradigm.

That paradigm rests on several key principles but the core of it is this:

You cannot control if, how, or when something great is going to happen to you.

You cannot predict the future.

You cannot control if your customers will buy.

You cannot control if your company will promote you.

You cannot control if someone will fund your startup.

But you can control what you do every single day. Every single hour. Your choice is under your control. And it will be your choices that will make you luckier.

That's the heart of Making Your Own Luck: focusing your efforts at controlling what you do every day and not just relying on waiting for things to happen to you.

That luck paradigm is a recipe that follows not ingredients but behaviours you can use in accelerating the chances of your success.

Throughout our careers—at the top of Corporate America in New York City to the top of a billion-dollar startup scene rapidly changing India—we have witnessed personal challenges, setbacks, obstacles, failures, triumphs and success. We have met and done business for over fifty collective years on so many levels. And what we have learned will surprise you.

We believe that you cannot wait for luck to happen.

Neither can we simply just "work hard". That's simply not going to be enough.

You Must Own It.

We believe that in our new hyper-accelerated and super competitive world, you must make your own luck.

Whether you're looking for the ideal job, trying to boost sales in your territory or come up with billion-dollar startup ideas or find new ways to grow your business, these seven luck accelerators can take you to new heights.

While randomness and chance play an important role in the world of startups and the world of sales and a corporate career, you can increase the odds of success in your favour. We believe that luck shouldn't be left up solely to chance but shaped day in and day out by the driving force that moves the world forward: choice.

The choices you make in your life right now—by reading this book, by putting to work the tools and principles of this book into practice in your everyday life—will put you on a path of success in your workplace, in your career, in your business, in your startup, and in your life.

The hand you've been dealt in life doesn't determine whether you'll win or lose. It is the way you play the hand that will determine your future. It is the choices you make that will determine your success in life. It will be based on your ability to call upon your internal discipline to own the luck accelerators that put your life on a rapid path to growth, prosperity, contribution, and success.

We believe that your best years lie ahead of you. Luck,

chance, and opportunities in your startup, your career, and your life have an incredible opportunity to accelerate by following these principles.

The Path to Success is made up of choices and chances, not recipes or formulas. And most importantly, remember that these choices are under our control.

This book will help you figure out how.

You will learn how to best position your life, your startup, your career, your sales efforts and your business for massive success.

You don't have to be lucky. You have to be passionate.

Stop waiting for luck to come into your life.

Start making your own luck.

We will share with you what we have learnt.

Bob Miglani   **Rehan Yar Khan**

CHAPTER 1

BE OBSESSIVELY CURIOUS

Curiosity is the spark behind luck, chance, and randomness, greatly improving your odds of success in life. Curiosity is the engine behind innovation in helping you find opportunities in a crowded market full of mediocrity. It is the origin of ideas, solutions, and products that have built successful companies and turned many people into multi-millionaire entrepreneurs and captains of industry.

Here's the winning pattern: curiosity leads to learning. Deep learning leads to knowledge. Knowledge leads to understanding. Understanding leads to connecting the dots. Connecting the dots rapidly accelerates your luck.

Ola Cabs is one of the most successful startups in the world. Launched about the same time as Uber in the US, its business model has been validated, lauded, and celebrated. Looking back at my initial investment round of $100,000 which, at one point, turned into a valuation of $75 million, it seems quite obvious that funding in Ola was a no-brainer.

But the real question is not whether it was the right or wrong investment. The real question is: how I ended up meeting Ola's founder and deciding to invest in it at a time when no one wanted to.

For many, it's easy to dismiss my investment as lucky. That it was simply a matter of a chance meeting and random favourability towards agreeing to invest.

But was it?

We believe it's deeper than that. We believe the answer to that question leads us to uncover one of the most important secrets of rapidly boosting the level of success in your life and that is:

Be Obsessively Curious – Rehan

In order to fully understand how this luck accelerator called curiosity made me lucky enough to generate millions on a $100,000 investment, we have to dig underneath the surface.

Somewhere in the spring of 2009, as my own startup Flora2000 was doing well, I started running into other entrepreneurs and with a few of them formed the Mumbai chapter of the Indian Angel Network (IAN). With other like-minded entrepreneurs, I began to lay the foundation for what I had hoped would become a vibrant ecosystem for startup founders to gain insight, knowledge, and experience to help grow the angel investment scene in Mumbai. As my name spread as a successful entrepreneur and an angel investor, I started to get introductions from people who were interested in pitching me to fund their startups.

One of those introductions was to a startup called Redbus. Referred to me by a friend, the startup founder was seeking an angel investment to launch the company into the mobility space in India. Redbus did something very interesting at the time. It listed the trips of multiple intercity bus operators on the internet allowing bus travellers to book a seat online. So, if someone wanted to travel from Chandigarh to Delhi for instance, she would simply go to Redbus and book her seat on a bus that took her from one city to another. Fairly simple but at the time very unique. No one was really in that space. I was intrigued by the idea of intercity travel because India has a large market of approximately 100 million domestic tourists a year who travel via train, air, bus, and car, so it was a large addressable market, growing well.

This was the first company I had come across in the people mobility space and only then did I fully realise how large the mobility space was as a potential business opportunity. People had to move around, every day. That's what populations today do—move from one place to another.

As I began to evaluate the pitch from Redbus, my curiosity took hold of me and didn't let go. Intrigued by how people get around in India, I did some initial research trying to read whatever I could about the mobility market. There were only a few marketplace studies so I had to pull from a large cross-section of sources. I stayed awake at night asking myself questions I didn't have answers to. How many people walk a day? How many actually travel from one city to another? What were various modes of transport and who used what? How do people really get around? What were the factors that lead people to choose one mode of transportation over another? Curious to learn more, I began my journey of deep learning.

Luck Byte

Learn. Get deeply immersed in a specific area, even if it doesn't have a compelling reason for a short return on investment. Because unique opportunities are not found in the market where everyone is already playing. Unique opportunities are found when you're on the search for knowledge and understanding.

I started to study the entire mobility industry trying to understand how things work. What were the various "cuts" in mobility? Intercity, intracity, mass transit, walking, private transport, motorbiking, cycling, etc. I put together this chart on a spreadsheet and tried to figure out how times a year people move around. It might have been crazy but I couldn't help myself because I didn't want just facts, I wanted to understand everything in minute detail.

As part of this process, I also learned about the various parts of the mobility industry—everything ranging from automobile manufacturing to fleet-owning cab companies and the driver industry. It was as I had suspected, a largely underserved market.

One important factor I learned, which would come in useful several times in the future, was about yield management. On any transportation vehicle, such as an aircraft, car, bus, etc., the mortgage cost, monthly maintenance, and staff cost (drivers and crew) are fixed. Fuel and tyres are the major variables. Thus, the more a vehicle is in revenue generating use, the more profitable it is. The secret to running a transport business such as a bus service, an airline, a cab company, etc. is generating the utmost yield from the asset by keeping vehicles in maximum use. So that's why, for instance, airlines like to turn around planes at the airport as fast as possible. Because the more they fly, the higher the yield.

Over the course of three months, I became an obsessive student again and learned all I could about mobility in India. To really understand, I had to go deeper than a superficial reading or assessment. My curiosity forced me to not only do robust academic desk research but to pursue a quest for real-world understanding as I reached out for advice and insight from anyone who knew anything about the mobility space including fleet operators who had a wealth of experience to share. In one particular meeting with limo operators who operated intercity routes, I learned that 90% of their business comes from 10% of their customers, mostly local businessmen.

On the public taxi front, I enjoyed using Meru, a new cab company in India, which sent you nice cabs when you called them. They were a huge relief from the black and yellow cabs available in Mumbai, which were unprofessional, unsafe, and could not be called by phone. In the back of my mind, I got the sense that the taxi business could become very large in India as there was tremendous latent demand for professional cabs.

I picked up the phone and made a cold call to speak to the CEO of Meru, who graciously agreed to spend some time with me educating me about the mobility market. It was the first national cab company that brought a higher level of standardisation to its product offering. After speaking with the CEO, I realised Meru was an asset-heavy model because they would own all their cars. Was it the right approach to mobility, to own your assets? Was there a role for an "asset-light" model that I had learned to do earlier? Further, what could algorithmic technology achieve? I wasn't sure until I started making the deeper connections to my past experience of building Flora2000.

Luck byte

Do not be afraid to call successful people.

Connecting Flora2000 to Mobility

In 2004, I had set up an online floral gifting company, which after several pivots in the business model had become an online florist for people who wanted to send flowers internationally. It targeted the diaspora in the US for gifting back home, an audience the local floral majors had not focused on. Flora2000 provides an online catalogue of 180+ countries, where we create the floral composition and shoot them in our studios. Customers choose what they wish to send and it can be delivered as early as the same day, worldwide.

On the supply side in each country, we have one of our partners, who assemble bouquets as per our design instructions and then deliver them. When customers come and shop on our website, orders go into our complex computer system, using algorithms which relays the order to the right partner, taking into account time zones, local holidays, language, weather conditions, etc. The partner delivers the flowers and enters the delivery details into our system. Our system immediately informs the customer. Accounting, product management, customer service, etc. are all built into this one large system.

So, here's the thing: Flora2000 runs a large online florist business with no florist shop. We don't buy, stock, or deliver flowers. Our insight, when starting the business, at all times even before the pivots was that there are enough florists in the world, so the business opportunity is not in creating another florist shop but in creating a brand, marketing it, and coordinating the ecosystem to build a successful floral business. It was an "asset-light" model.

Understanding Mobility

The more I learned about the topic of mobility spurred on by my curiosity, the more I began to understand where the opportunities lay and also what I should avoid. As a result of my initial research, I decided not to invest in Redbus, because at that time it was a low gross margin business, with just 1% margin and I was uncertain if there were other possibilities to grow the bottom line.

Redbus later sold for $140 million, so possibly I would have made a large return. **There was an important lesson I learnt from this and other such misses is that if there is a phenomenal founder behind the startup, he/she will figure out a way to make the company successful.** Today when I invest in the early stages, my greatest considerations are the team and space, and not only the present business model.

Redbus sparked my curiosity. My mind fed on it, to begin the process of deep learning and understanding the mobility market.

Meeting Ola

In November 2010, about nine months after my initial deep dive into mobility, I was invited to participate in a small conference, as a speaker. A handful of young founders clutching their business plans full of dreams were circling the room for investors. Later, as I was standing in line at the buffet and somewhere between the salad and the main course, the event organiser came up to me along with a vibrant and serious young guy, named Bhavish Aggarwal.

He introduced Bhavish to me asking him to speak with me about his "cabs" business. We decided to get lunch together and he started telling me about the business, hoping that I would become the first investor in Ola. Initially, I was not very interested as Meru had been around for many years, was well funded, and was much liked. Having done thorough research on Meru, I had known this already. But then he said something that piqued my interest. "We don't want to buy cabs. There are one million tourist vehicles in India, what we want to do is to network them."

As he said those words, something sparked inside my mind and struck a chord, re-igniting all I had learned during my deep dive of curiosity almost a year back. My ears perked up. Knowing how fast we had built Flora2000, I knew this notion of connecting the existing supply in the market was a magic formula. Conceivably, they could build a large taxi business using the already existing supply.

What also mattered to me was that Bhavish and his partner had studied computer science, a critically important expertise, because my back of the envelope calculations showed that this could be a large market of more than a 20 million to 30 million rides a day only if someone could crack the algorithm for managing all the vehicles effectively. It would take a lot of algorithmic work to coordinate millions of dynamic supply and demand nodes at this massive scale. This algorithm was important because it needed to be very good at ensuring Ola would get a high yield on its vehicles, which is the key to success in the transportation business.

All the studying, researching, going out to meet operators and heads of taxi businesses was coming in handy. My deep domain knowledge from almost a year ago had prepared me for that moment of chance.

Being "asset-light", having the possibility of high yield management, connecting a large supply of already existing vehicles, much like we had done at Flora2000 and the founders' expertise in building a sophisticated system were all the key factors that led me to decide on making an investment. I was in.

However, it turned out that I was the only one who wanted to invest in Ola Cabs. Though the initial round was just over $100,000, no one else wanted to put in any money. People said "Yaar, I can wave my hand and get a taxi", or "Meru's already there". As I helped Bhavish raise money, I tried to explain to those potential investors that Ola Cabs was an "Asset-Light" model, but they would not listen.

Finally, my friend Anupam Mittal listened and decided to invest one-third; I convinced my mother to invest and together, we ended up putting in two-thirds of the $100K. It was actually an unwise angel investment as we all were taking on a lot of risk, doing such large chunks of the round, but I wanted to get these passionate kids the money. That $100K today is worth close to $75 million, a 1000x return!

Note: Some people believe Ola was a copy of Uber, but back then, neither the founders nor we, as investors had heard of Uber. The fact is that I made the angel investment in Ola a few months after Uber had raised its angel round on the other side of the world and before it raised its seed round.

Lucky with Ola

Though it looks like I got lucky with an investment in Ola Cabs, it was a journey which began almost fourteen years ago in 2004, when I started Flora2000. The profitable surplus of Flora2000 helped me become an angel investor. The insight from Flora2000 on being "asset-light" helped shape my thinking about the market for Ola. But many entrepreneurs were looking at the asset-light model of business and lots of people had $100,000 to invest in Ola. But they didn't. So, the real key to my luck was not just starting and successfully running Flora2000. The real spark of making my own luck came when I began to be passionately curious.

The reason deep learning is important to speeding up luck is because it gives us insight, ideas, experiences, and an understanding that doesn't come so easily floating on the surface.

Breaking out of mediocrity requires us to raise the level of understanding to a plane of mastery. So many people accept the basic information that is provided to them and don't think about asking more detailed questions. They lose the opportunity to up their game. They ignore an opportunity to raise their standards.

Most others are not going to explore an issue or problem in serious depth and so the ones who do will generate unique breakthroughs about customers, understand what might work in the marketplace, and what might be the missing opportunities where their product or business could make a dent.

Armed with a deeper understanding we are also more likely to gain friends, partners, associates, or investors who believe in our cause.

Since and before Ola, I have made many more successful investments by studying an industry deeply. I invested in Druva when no one wanted to invest in another "backup" company; I invested in Country Delight because I found their model unique amongst all dairy businesses out there. Altogether in the past 10 years—2008 to 2018—I have been able to invest in around fifteen unique and special companies, that have gone on to become market leaders.

Curiosity creates a complex and intricate web of neurons in our minds, helping us learn and understand information at a subconsciously deep level. Being curious opens up our mind to new learning, new contacts and makes our mind more fertile for new ideas to develop.

Curiosity leads us down a path of discovery uncovering hidden jewels of opportunity.

Having a deep desire to learn for the sake of understanding, not for the sake of money, helps us to uncover opportunities that can create great prosperity and success later on, not only in the world of startups but in growing a successful career in the corporate world.

Curiosity Accelerates Success in Corporate Career – Bob

I was twenty-two years old, had no money, had just graduated from college, and needed to find a job. I was told that it was a tough economy with the economic recession. "Jobs are hard to find these days, Bob," people told me. At a conference I attended, I heard a business leader say to us, the hungry students, "I know you've been told that there are not a lot of jobs out there. But I want to tell you something very important. Listen closely. You don't need a lot of "jobs" . . . you only need to find one."

With a smile on my face and a positive attitude, I got busy looking for a job in sales. I had decided to look for any job but my focus was the pharmaceutical industry because I had heard they paid well and were global companies. I always had this vision of myself working in the international division of a big global company.

After several months of searching, I was staring at a pile of rejection letters that were gathering dust on my small wooden desk in my parents' humble house in the suburbs of New Jersey. I was tired. Tired of being rejected and told I was too young or too inexperienced. I was starting to get frustrated and angry and blamed the business world and the system for not giving me a chance.

As I started to stare in frustration at my desk, the rejection letter on top of the pile of letters caught my eye. I noticed it was from a company called Pfizer Inc. in New York City. It read something like this:

"Dear Bob:

Thank you for applying for the position of Sales Representative with our company. While we appreciate your application, we cannot offer you an interview at this time due to your lack of experience for this position. We wish you good luck in your future."

Sincerely,
Hank Allen
Vice President of Sales"

I stared at the letter and noticed a phone number at the very bottom of the letter. It was the phone number that must have been included in the template and a curious thought occurred that moment: Why don't I call him?

Don't be ridiculous, my mind shouted back. You can't just call him. You'll embarrass yourself. You're nobody. He's the head of sales for this big company.

As I was about to be discouraged and delete that thought of calling him, another curious thought appeared in my mind: What's the harm? What do you have to lose?

Full of hope that the simple question filled me with, I picked up the house phone in our kitchen and called the number at the bottom of the letter. No planning. No rehearsal. Not thinking about what I was going to say. Just called.

I was twenty-two years old, didn't have a job, did have a rejection letter, and worked at the ice-cream shop of Indian immigrants who were trying to survive in the world. And I called the Vice President of Sales at Pfizer.

The phone rang and the secretary picked up.

May I speak to Mr Allen please, I asked.

Who's calling, please?

Hi, my name is Bob Miglani and I am calling to speak with Mr Allen.

What is this about, may I ask?

I would like to speak to Mr Allen about an interview.

How did you get our number, may I ask?

Well, he sent me this very nice letter and his phone number was at the bottom of the page.

What letter did you receive? What did it say?

With a smile, I read her the letter informing her that it was a rejection letter.

Well, honey, I'm sorry but I can't help you. He sent you that letter already.

OK. Thank you very much, Ma'am. I hung up the phone.

I was disappointed. But still, I was overcome with this little bit of joy. I had done it. I called. I hadn't been afraid. I had done it. Thrilled at doing this simple task, I couldn't wait to try it with someone else.

But just then I realised that if I could call her once, why not call her again?

And so, over the course of the next three or four weeks, I called the secretary of the vice president of sales at Pfizer, asking her day in and day out to speak to him. I said, just give me a chance ma'am. I only want an interview. I'll work for free. I just want a shot. Only an interview—I told her time and time again.

Weeks went by and she got to know me well and started to anticipate my calls. Until one day, instead of saying no, she said yes. She said YES! I got on the phone for five minutes with the head of sales and asked him for an interview. He said, you know, you've been pretty persistent with my secretary and I can't say no to that. You have an interview in one month's time. Show up in our regional office in New Jersey at 8.00 a.m. on Friday and you'll have that interview.

I had done it. I was able to get an interview for a sales job at Pfizer. Even after being rejected.

Now I had to prepare.

Curiosity is the spark. It gets you in the door.
You have to walk through it prepared.
It is fuelled by learning.

I had a clear goal: get a sales job at Pfizer. It wasn't easy because in 1992, Pfizer didn't hire anyone just out of college. It wasn't going to be an easy interview. I was excited, thrilled, nervous, and didn't know where to begin.

Luck byte

Nothing focuses your work like
a clear and distinct goal.
Make your goal as specific and
compelling as possible.

Again, my curiosity led me to ask, "What kind of person do they want to hire? What skills or traits would that person have? If it is a strong salesperson, then what are the skills that all successful salespeople have?"

Luck byte

Remember, curiosity is not about me—it's about them. What do they need? What do they want? What makes a great salesperson? I didn't ask: What should I put on my resume? What knowledge should I have on the company? Because that's basic. But to be obsessively curious: learn and dig deeper on a more fundamental level. I asked: What makes a salesperson great?

So, I started at the public library (this was the pre-internet era). I set out on a journey to learn. Learn about what it took to be a super successful sales rep. To be a winner in the field of sales. I started reading books and journals and researching articles written by the best authors and experts in the field of sales.

Each evening, on the way back home from working at my parents' ice-cream shop, I stopped at the public library and stayed there until closing time. In between serving customers and cleaning the floors, I read books in the back of the shop about behaviours and traits of successful salespeople. I read all about the pharmaceutical industry. About Pfizer and its competitors.

In preparation for the interview, I threw myself into deep learning and started to understand the core behaviours and traits of successful salespeople. I took lots of notes and filled more than three notebooks with ideas and examples of how salespeople became successful. Ideas on persistence, communication skills, adapting to the customers' needs, determination, positive attitude, and more. I didn't realise it at the time but investing that time studying provided me with a crucial knowledge of success I had never been taught.

On one sheet of paper, I summarised the ten or fifteen traits that I had collected through reading thirty or more books over the course of the four weeks leading to the interview.

Instead of just printing out a resume, I created a presentation that was titled, "Top 10 Reasons to Hire Bob Miglani". Each of the ten slides contained one trait that was important in successful salespeople. And under each point, I listed bullet points of how I learned these behaviours and traits based on my experience working in my family's ice-cream shop or during my college days.

It was essentially a sales presentation on why they should hire me. It took countless hours studying for one interview for one hour.

The Interview

On the day of the interview, I was nervous but never more prepared in my life. The interviewer was a man named Bob Miller, who was the District Sales Manager for Pfizer in Manhattan. He had recently been promoted to Sales Manager after fifteen years working as a successful sales rep himself in New York City. He was not only knowledgeable and smart, but he was also charismatic and brutally honest. He was a tough New Yorker, born and raised in the city.

After exchanging some initial pleasantries, we began the interview. He began with the basic question "Tell me about yourself". I answered in an unusual way. I said I had prepared a presentation for him and would like to present it. He didn't mind and asked me to go ahead.

I told him that in preparation for this interview, I had studied long and hard about what it takes to be a successful salesperson and read many books and came up with the top ten traits. I shared these with him and asked, "Would you agree that these 10 traits are very important to be a successful salesperson?" He answered yes and I started my presentation.

I explained how, over the course of my life, as short as it had been at the time, I had gained these exact traits through my experience in life, highlighting the specific trait and the bullet points that went with it.

For instance, I learned the trait "excellent communication skills" through working at my family's ice-cream shop, interacting with customers, training the other staff and also dealing with suppliers and vendors who were older than me.

As I went through each trait, I tried my best to explain how I had these traits within me waiting to come out to serve. At the end of my presentation, I summed up by asking him, "So, Mr Miller, would you agree that I demonstrated that I have the skills and traits to be a successful salesperson?" He answered, "Yes".

"So, do I get the job?" I asked, politely but firmly.

He smiled and said, "I like what you're doing. Closing me. But I haven't asked you anything yet. Why don't I ask you a few questions and then we can figure out the answer to your very good close?" he stated.

We went through another half hour or so of questions and at the end, I asked him if he would give me the job.

He told me that he couldn't tell me right away because he wanted me to meet with someone else that morning.

After waiting for a couple of hours, I met with his regional manager and proceeded to present my case as I had done hours before ending with the same question: Do I get the job?

Both smiled and said, we'll let you know in a few days and thanked me with a firm handshake and bid me goodbye.

I left the Pfizer regional office exhausted that Friday afternoon. I headed home with a feeling of satisfaction that I had done all I could, although I was a little disappointed that they didn't give me a yes right away.

At about 8.00 p.m. that night, I received a call from the District Sales Manager, Mr Bob Miller, offering me the job. I couldn't believe it. Without asking for the details of the offer, I accepted the job immediately with a feeling of joy and happiness.

I had done it. I had gotten a job at Pfizer, that too in the time of recession, difficult competition, and great odds. In a week's time, I received the official offer letter from the company. Only a few months ago, I had held the rejection letter from this company in the same hand. A poor Indian kid in America who had worked at his family's ice-cream shop had gotten a shot at a professional job in a global company.

The lesson in this story is that curiosity is nothing grand and mysterious. It is fairly simple and requires neither money nor connections nor any other resources but an eager mind willing to listen to the question that many of us think about: What if?

What if I call that number?

What if I keep calling?

What if I actually get an interview?

What is it they want?

What's the secret of successful salespeople?

What does the customer really want?

How can I serve better?

These questions were what I was after, and trying to understand the answer is what led me to be "lucky" enough to get my first job with Pfizer. And the same curiosity helped me to become a #1 sales rep in a field of thousands, to grow into other roles at Pfizer, create new departments, rapidly boosting my career in the one of the largest companies in the world.

Summary

Be obsessively curious. Curious about how things work.

Explore "what if" moments, "why not?" thoughts.

Let the curiosity of life and business lead you down a path of exploration, discovery, and understanding.

Ask. Read. Call people. Stop wasting time watching TV and get busy reading and learning about life.

Follow that spark of curiosity quickly because it only flashes for a second. Be alert to it and follow it down the rabbit hole.

Leave the outside world behind and follow the light down the dark hole of learning.

Be consumed not by the notifications on your cell phone or social media but by the desire to learn.

It will be this path of knowledge and understanding that will allow you to have realisations, develop new ideas, uncover deep insights, begin new paths, meet new people and experience things that will build your character and accelerate your success.

Curiosity is not only asking a question—it's an attitude of expressing a deep desire to learn, if only for the sake of learning and experiencing.

Key Learnings

1. Dig your well long before you are thirsty: be prepared. Whether it is a job interview, an investment, a game in sports, or throwing a party, the most important thing you can do is be well prepared. Today, with the all the information on the internet, easy connectivity to people through chat applications like WhatsApp, and the millions of books available and plentiful access to professional coaching and education, it is a sin to start something without preparation.

   Learn. Find something you are interested in and get busy learning like you have never done before.

2. Be curious about people. Build a large and diverse network. Very often people either have a small external network or it's not diverse enough. Instead of only networking with people in business, get to know people from other walks of life: sports people, government employees, taxi drivers, the creative industry and many others.

   Anyone and everyone has something valuable to share. From the bus driver to the CEO, they all have insights to offer. When you meet people, ask them questions. What do they do? How did they grow up? Why do they do what they do? What is their secret to success? What motivates them? Build a broad network and keep it active. You can then reach out if you need advice, introductions, references, or assistance. A large network allows you to pick the mind of experts to increase your knowledge and experience.

I once met a man worth $10 billion. We met through common friends and were part of a dinner program where he had received an award for his humanitarian work. Throughout the three hours we spent together, he was warm, friendly, and obsessively curious. He had learned I worked at Pfizer and was curious about how the business worked. Where was the manufacturing done? How did they do their research? What was my job? He threw a thousand questions at me, with only one motive—to learn, to understand. Throughout that night, I noticed him being curious about everyone—from the celebrities to the waiters to the cleaning lady to the businesswoman who was CEO. He must have met several others. Think about what he must have learned from that one dinner party!

3. Use powerful words that accelerate your curiosity such as, "Yes", "Sure" "What if" "Why not?" Use these words to inquire and discover hidden secrets that lead you to riches. Attend a seminar in an industry you know nothing about. Ask someone about what they do and how they do it so well. Read a book about a subject

you know nothing about. Listen to a podcast on an uncomfortable subject.

Now, here's your action plan. Write down the answers to the three questions. Feel free to begin/end your day by reviewing it.

My Action Plan

1. What is the one area that I will commit to learning about deeply? Just for the sake of learning and understanding. List the one area here.

    ....
    ....
    ....
    ....

2. Have I built deep knowledge of a few areas, or am I a jack of all trades but master of none? What will I do daily to build my way up to attain mastery in a subject area?

    ....
    ....
    ....
    ....

3. Who are the three people I will call this week to ask them about advice or insight?

    ....
    ....
    ....
    ....

CHAPTER 2

GIVE. CREATE VALUE. SOLVE A PROBLEM FOR OTHERS.

Many of us struggle with answering this question—the wrong one—that haunts us during our journey of finding success: How do I make money?

In pursuit of luck and success, that's the wrong question to ask. Yes, we need money and financial success to provide for ourselves and our loved ones. But the question "how do I make money?" leads us down the road chasing after the wrong path that never lead us to financial success.

Instead, the more important question to ask is: "Who can I serve?" "What problem can I solve with my gifts, talents, interests, and skills?" This is one of the most profound and powerful questions to ask yourself because the answer provides a more solid path to prosperity.

In this question lies a fundamental and universal truth: Give and you shall receive.

Some call it Karma. Others call it the Law of Reciprocity. Some confuse it with the Golden Rule. Whatever name you place on this well-known principle of life, it is a truth which has been recognised for generations by millions around the world.

When you give, you will receive.

Give without expecting anything in return.

But how does this apply to accelerating luck in the world of sales, startups, or a corporate career? What does karma have to do with boosting success?

The answer lies not in the stars but in something more down to earth: relationships.

Whether they're customers, business partners, prospects, friends, or family members, people make the world go round. Through the exchange of ideas, goods, and services people have created markets and institutions where the give and take of relationships rest as the foundational principle.

People's decisions, choices, and perceptions have an impact on your growth. Whether you're trying to sell them something, asking them to invest, or working with them as a team on a big corporate project, the way you work with people matters immensely.

And people have problems. People have obstacles that are blocking their personal growth in their life, business, and career. People are facing challenges. People have needs, desires, and wants.

By helping other people solve their problem using your own gifts, talents, resources, or ideas, you create VALUE.

That value didn't exist before you created it.

Helping to create value in relationships is one of the most important aspects for accelerating growth. It doesn't matter if they are customer-company relationships or teacher-student relationships or friend to stranger relationships.

Using your energy, resources, creativity, connections, and effort, you help them. That problem was not solved before you got there. Their struggle was going unresolved. That change in the other person's life is VALUED because you did something.

Give. Contribute. Help. Support. Create Value.

People often confuse this idea of giving with the notion "I must give away my product. That's how I create value." Well, not really. They—the person, whether they're the customer, prospect, or your business partner—have a problem they don't know how to solve—and if you can help solve it, you will be creating value for them. Sometimes, the help you provide them will have nothing to do with your product or service.

And the second part of this principle is this: When value is created—it is returned.

In some way, shape, or form, the value will be returned to you. It may not be as crystal clear or immediate as you might hope, but you will be rewarded eventually. It may not be a **financial** reward but there will be something returned to you if your effort is valued. And it will come back to you in a nonlinear manner.

Druva: Contribution is Your North Star – Rehan

Around 2008, while running my startup Flora2000, I was a habitual visitor to various online forums.

My mindset was not as an investor but only as someone who had launched a startup that was doing well and was interested in learning more. I was curious to see if there were other people like me who were running startups and the one place I found online for Indian founders to talk was a forum called Venture Woods.

Excited to see what other people like me were thinking about and doing, I stumbled upon the thread where someone had posed a question about storage space for their website and desktop. It had something to do with being able to have a backup system for data. In those days, no one was talking about cloud backup but I discovered one response in particular that struck me as a very thoughtful answer to the question. This guy had answered it well. I remembered thinking at the time, "Wow, this guy gave a really good answer. He must know what he is talking about."

The guy who answered the question around backup for data was a young twenty-six-year-old named Jaspreet Singh. His response struck me as being detailed, thoughtful, and helpful to the person who posed the question. Struck by his valuable response, I sent him a private message to compliment him on his advice. He responded nicely and we started to get to know each other.

Through that online forum and later from phone calls here and there, I learnt that Jaspreet has recently quit his job, got together with some ex-colleagues and, had developed a way to implement server backup in real time. From my experience of running Flora2000 in 2008, server backup of non-database objects was cumbersome and I thought Jaspreet had an interesting solution to the problem. Along with his two colleagues, Jaspreet had come up with a way to do continuous backups without loading systems much. They had invented "light footprint continuous data protection".

Jaspreet hadn't come to me for funding or advice. We just happened to meet because he had offered something of value to someone who had a problem. Impressed with his idea and the way he was thinking about backup, after a few conversations over the phone, I offered to help introduce him and his co-founders to a few of my friends for investment (as we wanted to raise some money).

Forming the Indian Angel Network (IAN)

At the time, I didn't think of myself as an angel investor, nor did it occur to me that I could invest in Druva. I was consumed with running my own startup. Simply put, I liked Jaspreet. He had a good idea that I wanted to see be used out in the world. He was a good guy with a good idea. And I wanted to help out this really nice guy.

Luck byte

Helping someone for the right reason is creating value of the highest order.

At the same time, it so happened that a group of people in Delhi had formed an angel network called Band of Angels and invited me to join as a very early member (the network was later renamed to Indian Angel Network).

I called Jaspreet to tell him that I was going to get him into a pitch session that the Indian Angel Network was setting up, to which he inquired, "What is angel investing?". I didn't know exactly what it was either but explained that it was a way for him to get funding for his idea.

Having never seen his business plan, I went with him to the Indian Angel Network pitch in New Delhi. Accompanied by his father, I could tell Jaspreet was a bit nervous as the potential funding could lead to a big change in his life.

While waiting for Jaspreet to get ready to do the pitch, I got to meet his father. An Ex Indian Army man, Jaspreet's father expressed his reservation at the son's quest for entrepreneurship. "I worry about what he's doing. He left a good job recently."

As luck would have it, Jaspreet's pitch didn't impress the audience in the room that day. But I didn't want to let this idea die on the vine. It was too good and Jaspreet was such a nice guy. I wanted to help. I volunteered to become the "deal lead" for the network and champion raising money for Druva. Over the next few weeks, I called a number of network members to see if they'd be interested. As I mentioned earlier, I hadn't even seen the business plan but was compelled to help this guy bring a good idea to the market.

In total, there were only seven of us who invested as angel investors, amounting to about US$200,000. I was the lead investor and took the board seat. Despite the business and technical challenges that go along with any startup, Jaspreet and his co-founders, through several pivots and setbacks, were able to create what is one of the most successful software product companies to come out of India till date. Which brought tremendous rewards for investors like me and my co-investors, where the initial $200,000 investment seeded a company that has gone on to become worth more than $1 Billion. But the bigger reward for me was that I was able to help a really good guy bring a really good product to market. A product that adds value to businesses across the world.

The chance of luck in Jaspreet's life increased by 3x at the very moment he answered a question posed by someone in an online forum. He helped someone. The odds of my luck increased by 10x at the moment I decided to help Jaspreet find people who would invest in his idea. The value I had provided was in helping him secure funding even though I had no plans to become an investor. It was only when there was a need for a lead investor did I step up and raise my hand.

Giving service and helping others is a major contributor for increasing success in life because your effort creates value. And once value is created, it will be reciprocated in some way or other in a way that we cannot predict or control. But it will be returned to you.

People often make the mistake of saying, "I want to start a company", when instead, they should be saying, "What problem can I solve? Who can I serve? What value can I create for this specific person?" That's the secret of increasing success in your startup or in your career.

How Can I Help Dr Thomas? – Bob

When I was a sales rep for Pfizer Inc. in New York City, my sales territory was lower Manhattan which encompasses a large and diverse group of customers including doctors in Chinatown, hospitals in Greenwich Village and clinics in the Lower East Side. Rich with cultural diversity, traffic, and excellent hospitals and doctors, it was sometimes difficult to understand how I should approach growing the business I was given.

I was promoting a very important product to doctors in Chinatown but was having difficulty in realising success even though I was working hard at understanding my product and the benefits over my competition. Studying clinical data, looking at market trends, researching the competition, analysing data and insurance benefits—all of it so that I could be really good at positioning my product in the right way with customers.

One day, a new doctor named Dr Thomas moved into one of the buildings right in the middle of the busiest locations in Chinatown. He had a large staff, good office space, and was well trained in his speciality having recently leaving the pulmonary residency program at a nearby hospital. Even though he had very few patients and thus was not a high priority for the business during the first few months, I went in to say hello to him to introduce myself, my company and the products I was promoting.

During our conversation, Dr Thomas was engaging, very thoughtful, and asked excellent questions about my product. He had some experience with the product while he was working in the hospital so was convinced of the value it provided. After our initial meeting, I left thinking what a pleasant man he was—smart, with a nice office, and engaging. If I was a patient that needed his service, I would certainly go to him. I sincerely wished him well and much luck in his practice.

On my next sales call that day with another doctor whom I had known for some time, I happened to mention my introductory meeting with Dr Thomas earlier. This doctor seemed curious to learn more and I was happy to provide more details. As I was talking about Dr Thomas' nice practice, his training and speciality, I realised that instead of promoting my product, I was promoting him. But it felt right because Dr Thomas was a kind man and I wanted to see him do well.

Over the course of the next few months, my enthusiasm for Dr Thomas only grew as I got to know him better. His sincerity was evident in the way he treated not only his patients but also his staff and the salespeople who often visited him. Since I visited doctors in the area often, I became a passionate advocate for Dr Thomas and his practice. I invited him to events, giving him an opportunity to meet other doctors and introduced him to doctors who had been in town for decades.

Those introductions created value for him because it

helped him get known and eventually gain valuable referral patients for his speciality. My introductions and enthusiastic advocacy of Dr Thomas helped him grow his practice. And over time, as his practice grew, so did his use of the product I had been promoting.

My sales grew dramatically in that year because I slowly realised the most important lesson in accelerating sales success:

No one cares about me.

No one cares about my idea, my product, my service.

No one cares about what I am trying to do.

They care about themselves. Their jobs. Their business. Their family.

It's not about me. It's not about you.

It's about them.

It's about the customer.

It's about what THEY need.

Not what *we think* they need.

Not what we think they will get out of our product. It's about helping them solve a problem. It's about contributing in some way to helping them achieve their goals by using resources, connections, ideas, or advocacy that are available to us. In this case, Dr Thomas needed referrals from other doctors and I could provide him introductions to doctors who could give him those referrals. It wasn't an arrangement. It was a natural occurrence that often happens when you're trying to do good for others.

We become successful the moment we realise that we need to help other people fulfil their needs and wants. Yes, we must have a good product or service that is important to them. But when we focus on someone else's needs and work on fulfilling that need—value is created.

> **"You can have anything in life that**
> **you want if you just help other people**
> **get what they want."**
> **-Zig Ziglar**

Developing a Business around Helping Others

From 2007 to about 2010, I went through a harrowing experience during my career at Pfizer Inc. The world's financial economy was under threat of collapsing, the business environment was getting more competitive, people were getting laid off, businesses were being shut down, banks were in a mess, and life became uncertain. After years of success and fulfilment in my career, I found myself on the verge of losing my job, being fearful of change, and slipping down a spiral of anxiety and self-doubt.

Amid the corporate reorganisation in Pfizer, I was falling apart mentally and confused, worrying about my job. I got a phone call from a friend who asked for my help. He wanted to go to India for the first time for a business project and wanted me to accompany him to help make introductions and show him around. I wasn't in any mood to take vacation time because of the uncertainty of losing my job but when he pleaded with me. I said "Yes" because I was trying to be helpful.

During that trip to India with my friend and seeing India through his eyes I came to the realisation that life is always uncertain and always changing. We cannot stop change. We cannot control it nor can we run from it. We have to move forward. We have to embrace it.

That realisation was profound and it helped me grow, change my life, and became the foundation for discovering a whole new career. After returning from that trip to India, I began the journey of reinventing my job and grew in my career, finding more success and more meaning in my life. I started a small blog where I shared my experiences with others who I thought might benefit from my learnings on how to deal with change and uncertainty. From one reader to thousands, the lessons on learning to deal with change became useful for those who were going through a difficult time coping with change in their own lives. They valued my ideas and stories.

Then one day, I was working on my computer in a hotel lobby in Ahmedabad when I saw a message from one of my readers—a message I will never forget. It made me emotional. It hit me right in the heart. I realised that someone was benefitting from my life experience.

She shared her life story which contained tragedies and circumstances surrounding the lives of many of us around the world. But her point in writing to me was to let me know that she valued my words. She appreciated what I wrote because it helped calm her and gave her perspective, insight, and freedom. It lightened her burdens in life because she realised she wasn't alone in carrying them. There were others. There was me, who not only shared my story but also provided some ideas on how to move forward. She encouraged me to continue writing because it was helping her stay motivated through difficult circumstances.

Whatever I was doing—some of it—was helping someone.

And there might be others.

As my blog became popular, I started turning it into stories and advice that would eventually form the basis of my bestselling book, *Embrace the Chaos*, which was published in 2013. Following its publication and my writing on my blog and other platforms, I started to receive requests to speak at companies to help their employees who were struggling with dealing with change. I slowly started to realise there was value in the lessons from my own journey for companies who were going through change and were in need of inspiration to help their employees move forward.

I didn't quit my job right away. As I evaluated my own purpose in life and how I might best serve others, I eventually left my corporate career at Pfizer Inc.—one of the biggest companies in the world. Today, I've built a career helping people embrace change and companies adapt to change and uncertainty. One of my jobs is to help creative people in these companies discover the brilliant ideas in their minds, nurture them and get them launched in the marketplace.

I was able to shift and grow my life and my career and create a whole new business, by simply helping other people embrace change and move forward. The universe put in motion a series of events that led me out of corporate America to start a whole new business in that moment of saying "Yes" to my friend who needed help on his business trip to India.

A career reinvention at Pfizer, a blog, a book, and a new business consultancy and speaking career were born the moment I said Yes to help someone and continued to flow forward in all the moments I served others—the readers of my blog, the readers of my book, and the audience invited to hear me speak.

Summary

Luck is accelerated when value is created. We define true value not as something that you think you should receive, but as something you CREATE. And it is something that you give to someone. It's what THEY need for a problem they are trying to solve or a desire they wish to obtain.

It's about them, not about you. If you want to speed up the level of success in your life, find out what people want and find a way to give it to them. Give with the intention to help. Contribute your time and resources not because you'll get something in return—because that's never a guarantee in this lifetime—but because it will help solve a problem. Becoming a problem solver is an incredible booster of luck and success. It helps you grow. It increases your chance of success. You accelerate your odds if you do.

Key Learnings

1. Be observant. Ask, inquire, and learn what's going on around you with an understanding of what problems exist in people's lives. In casual conversations when

someone mentions something apparently minor, don't dismiss it. Ask them about it.

2. Identify a problem that is going unanswered today. Don't think about the solution instantly. Rather, ask really good questions about the problem. Get to the heart of it.

3. Talk to as many people as possible about the problem to see if it needs to be solved. Then explore solutions you can think of. Remember, it doesn't have to be rocket science. It can be simple. Remember Ola Cabs is in one sense a simple idea—get a taxi.

My Action Plan

1. **Who is the one person I can help today? What are their needs? What is a problem that someone is trying to solve?**

....
....
....
....

2. **What ideas, resources, contacts do I have or actions I can take today to help them, knowing that I may never get anything back in return?**

....
....
....

3. **My commitment: By signing my name below, I dedicate my work to help improve the life of one other person. In my relationships with my family,**

friends, work colleagues, customers, and others, I will always do my best to contribute value to helping them with all the strengths, gifts, and talents I have. I recognise that value must first be created before it can be received. To this, I commit.

....

....

....

....

CHAPTER 3

DIVERGE. TAKE THE
ROAD LESS TRAVELLED

Be Unique. Find Your Niche. Be Different. Sail Uncharted Waters.

There is a temptation you must resist on your journey to success. Whether you're trying to climb the ladder in a corporate career or trying to break out into building your brand through your startup, you must fight the allure of following the herd.

Typically, when we think of our efforts to become successful, we tend to gravitate towards big numbers. Billions. Millions. We think of big market potential or market size. We think of big companies with large footprints globally. We think of joining the lucrative companies where everyone is heading.

We have a tendency to think big when we should ideally be thinking small. We should be thinking narrow.

Instead of following the herd, we should run in the opposite direction.

One of the most important lessons we have learned after decades in navigating the world of startups, big corporate careers and in life is this:

Be unique.
Be Different. Do something different.
Find Your Niche.
Sail uncharted waters.

By being unique and following a divergent path, you are more likely to stand out and become visible to your customers, to your boss, and to your audience.

Be a version of your true self. Pursue areas where there are fewer competitors. Challenge the norm. Dig out your own path. Chart your own individual course. Don't be like everyone else. Go into a market where you have a better chance to dominate.

Why? There are two parts to this principle.

The first is because your voice is more likely to be heard in a new market than one where you are one of countless voices in a crowded market screaming to be heard.

Whether you're standing in a queue at the restaurant, trying to move up in the corporate world or launch your startup - if you want to accelerate the chance of success, you have to get noticed.

And it is very difficult to get noticed when you're raising your hand among an ocean of competitors. Instead, we have found that it is better, at least initially to go into a newer more niched area where you have a better chance to dominate because there is fewer competition.

Second, divergence also allows you to find a niche or a domain of expertise that is ripe for opportunity. Going deep into that narrow domain offers you a chance to become an expert who would be valued by the marketplace, be it customers or your company.

"A tree does not grow in the shade of another."
-Rehan Yar Khan

Finding My Niche in the Flower Business – Rehan

I was born lucky.

No, I wasn't born into a family of wealth, prestige, or power. I was born into a hard-working family who gave me the best gift of all—a clean slate that allowed me to pursue any field where I could earn a living. My life was open to many possibilities, which left me somewhat confused in the early days but also quite open to exploring many different paths.

During my first couple of years in college, I studied hard but wasn't quite sure which path I was going to take. As my third year of college arrived the necessity to identify a field of endeavour became urgent because I knew my parents were going to pressurise me to find a job soon.

It was 1991 and I was studying economics at the time, learning about the changes in the Indian economy. Liberalisation was opening up the market for imports. The agriculture industry seemed like a good opportunity to get into, given that it was one of the biggest in India at the time. I figured that I could help these big agricultural companies from abroad come into India and as their agent, earning a fee from sales generated. My investment would be little to none with the potential for lucrative income because some of these big seed companies made a lot of money. My vision was to become a representative of those big companies for importing all agricultural products for the Indian market.

As the seed of an idea to become a sales agent grew in my mind, I became very excited and decided to travel to Europe to knock on the doors of some of those big agro companies. To my dismay, I got turned down by everyone.

I learned that I couldn't compete against the large sales agencies from India that were already in some kind of relationship with these big European or American agro companies, representing their big portfolio of agricultural products in India. No large company was going to give a third-year college student the rights to represent their agricultural seed products.

But in some of those early meetings, I discovered an opportunity that remained untouched by the hands of the big players: floral seeds. I learned that while the big companies would not allow a college student to represent them in India for their big agro products, they *would* take a chance on a college student to help them sell floral seeds in India. It was a comparatively smaller market, though it was huge in its own right as India was one of the world's largest growers of flowers and it gave me an opening I didn't have. So, I took a chance and became an agent selling floral seeds to farmers in India.

It was a good starting point for my entrepreneurial journey because I learned how to sell and manage relationships with large companies. For six years, from 1992 till about 1998, the business grew and did well. We became no.1 in the supply of bulbs, carnation plants, and chrysanthemum saplings. There is a good chance if you buy an Asiatic or Oriental Lily today in India, it came from the stock we sold back then.

Those days, travel was very different. There were no private airlines, only Indian Airlines (now merged with Air India) offering limited connectivity. So, I did a lot of bus travel, on STs (State Transport), which had wooden seats and three of us had to squeeze into the equivalent width of two economy class flight seats today, travelling for as much as sixteen hours at a time. I still remember the stops we would make at *dhabas* and have some of the most delicious food. It was amazing learning for a city boy like me travelling the length and breadth of rural India.

This was also a time when India had only about three million telephone lines in a country of nearly a billion people. It was a privilege to have a phone. In our office, we got our phone connection under the *Tatkal* system, whereby we had to pay a Rs.30,000 (US$1000+ back then). It also meant that most villages in India had no phones at all!

Though I was having a great time and rose to no.1 in the floral seed business and had enough money to stand on my own feet reducing any pressure from my parents to get a job, I wanted to do something that could grow faster. Since I didn't find buyers for the business at the time, I transferred the business to our various regional managers and exited.

When I called our foreign suppliers, I was paying Rs.70 (US$2+) per minute and when they called me, they were paying Rs. 3 (US$0.10). This got me thinking and I realised there could be an arbitrage opportunity here. So I started exploring and found that there was a way of using technology to legitimately route calls out of India on international leased lines. I went to work developing a supplier base for these lines.

From about 1998 to 2003, the arbitrage telecom business became high volume and it was highly profitable selling a subscription-based service to companies. There were other companies doing it as well, but we concentrated on Bombay and became no.1 in the city. There were BPOs, Foreign Banks, Multinationals, and others who lapped up our leased lines. I became good at sales. This was also my 1st tech business.

Then the telecom industry was privatised, starting with VSNL, followed by the cell phone revolution. Also, the Internet came along and services like Skype mushroomed. The arbitrage started disappearing and by 2003 it was nearly gone.

[Key learning: Every startup, every big company, every idea gets disrupted at some point. That's why it is important to consistently work hard on improving, innovating, and reinventing yourself and your business. You must constantly disrupt and diverge to stay ahead.]

It was the early 2000s and while I didn't see myself getting back into the import business, I did think about getting back into the floral business. What I had learnt was that the delivery part of flowers had high margins but fragmented competition. By consolidating the florists so that the consumer would have an easier way to send flowers, I thought there could be a good business. And so, in 2004, I started a company called Dial-a-Bouquet with the idea of having customers in the Mumbai area phone us to place their orders for flower delivery.

Very quickly I found out that this was a tough business because most people at the time were too shy to share their credit card details on the phone. Sending someone to collect money from the originator of the transaction was very expensive. I decided to either fold up and do something else or tweak the business in some way.

With the Internet starting to take off, I figured that people would feel secure punching in their credit card details online, as it would be a private transaction. I decided to rebrand the company as Flora2000 and focus selling only online and to serve all of India. We had a good infrastructure as we could deliver flowers anywhere in India which I hoped would turn into a compelling value proposition for customers.

As it turned out, I was wrong. Our infrastructure was good but trying to sell flowers online in India when there wasn't a culture of using credit cards to pay for merchandise was not a real business. We had built a very sophisticated operation with customised software and managed to consolidate floral delivery in such a complex country like India. But we didn't have many customers.

Then one day, thanks to Google we started receiving a few orders from the Indians who lived in the US to send flowers to their loved ones in India.

We didn't advertise on Google at the time but our website popped up during organic search results when someone in the US searched for flower delivery in India. This was something I hadn't expected and it changed the course of my business.

Looking into this, I realised that there was a small but genuine need for helping a customer in the US send flowers to someone in India. It wasn't about trying to become a floral delivery player in the US. Instead of trying to serve US customers for US flower deliveries and competing with the giants like 1-800-Flowers, I realised there was smaller, more niche market that the big players in the American floral delivery business were not serving: Americans, who were from someplace else in the world.

We were getting orders from Indian-Americans to deliver flowers to someone in India because there was no one else who could do that. Big online floral companies in the US were focused on serving local US customers doing

US deliveries. They weren't interested in making flower delivery into India. Yes, it was a much smaller market for us but one that we could serve exceptionally well given all the infrastructure we had developed for India. And even if we got a portion of the roughly two million Indians living in the US with credit cards in hand, who wanted to send flowers to their loved ones in India, this could be a decent market for us. But more importantly, this was a gap we could fill. We could do it exceptionally well. Yes, targeting the Indian Americans was a small market who wanted to send flowers to India but what about Germans? Brazilians? British? Or the thousands or potentially millions of immigrants living and working in the US who had relatives or friends back home in India.

Thinking about this, I realised that my startup, Flora2000, had potential. It wasn't the potential I had envisioned as an online floral delivery for the Indian market. It was different from that. But it would be ours to own. My startup could dominate in this space because there was no one else in it. Yes, the challenges of time zones, local addresses, seasonal availability of flowers, setting up the infrastructure from country to country would be extremely difficult, but those challenges would be there for everyone else too, and if we mastered them, they would become a *barrier to entry* for future competitors.

And we did.

We began a new and reinvigorated push to create a site that would serve American consumers who wanted to send flowers to countries around the world. First, we refined and uplifted our offering and infrastructure in India. Then we set up US to Mexico. Then US-Germany, US-Brazil, and other countries came quickly online after that.

By 2008, Flora2000 was a healthy and growing business delivering in 190 countries, serving millions of customers. We had our ups and downs like all startups but we had been serving a niche exceptionally well. With our sophisticated, customised software, strong relationships with suppliers, understanding of local time zones and cultures, local addresses, and an easy to use interface online, we had been able to dominate in an uncrowded market. By being different—being unique—finding and leading in a small but valuable niche, we were able to grow and succeed.

The success of Flora2000 provided me with the investment capital to begin my journey as an angel investor and eventually as a venture capitalist to some of the world class companies emerging in India.

What accelerated success in my own startup was that I was able to discover by accident—by luck—by chance—by getting doors slammed in my face—a valuable secret for startups: Be Unique.

We didn't take on the big boys in the seed import business.

In Telecom, we concentrated on Bombay—a city which others were not focusing on.

We didn't go head on with big competitors in the floral delivery business.

We came at all these businesses from the side.

There were unique angles that allowed us an opportunity to move forward in a new market where our voice had a high share.

Here's why being unique is really important in the world of startups: the destroyer of most startups isn't necessarily the lack of funding. Rather it is the enormous marketing expenses of trying to sell in a crowded market where the customer acquisition costs are very high.

Most startups have the gross margins figured out but often underestimate how much marketing they will have to do and spend precious resources to win customers. So, they get into a huge market thinking they'll get a small piece. But what happens is that they end up burning through funding too fast as they didn't think about how difficult and expensive customer acquisition can be with the bigger competitors dominating the market.

By focusing on a smaller, more specialised and narrower market, you have a better chance of being heard by the customers and people you wish to impress. Those precious impressions are often more meaningful, lucrative, and profitable.

The Concept of Divergence

Nature teaches us that over time, all sorts of species diverge—or become more specialised. Life evolves. The origin of life was from one cell, which over time diverged to two-cell and then an explosion of multi-celled organisms emerged on the plane of existence.

What started millions of years ago as one species of insects, today there are thousands of species with specific characteristics that while similar to their ancestors, embody qualities that are unique for the environment today.

Let's bring this closer to home.

If you consider restaurants in the 1950s in the US, there was essentially one kind—diners. Drive up with your car. Beep your horn and a waitress would come out, take your order, and deliver your food on a tray hooked up to your car's window. That was it. Then restaurants started diverging—or specialising. Burgers-only restaurants such as McDonald's started to appear which evolved to takeout. The coffee part of the diner became Starbucks. The chicken meals became Kentucky Fried Chicken. The pizza became Pizza Hut. Then over the last two decades, even these broad-based restaurants diverged even further. Pizza restaurants became more specialised offering deeper services and products such as home-deliver pizza (Dominos) offering a variety of toppings on pizza such as those offered by the California Pizza, Kitchen chain, frozen pizza (Barron's) and now going deeper into vegan, gluten-free and organic pizza.

The very first diner owner operating a restaurant in the 1950s could never have imagined the specialised varieties of food, flavours, concepts, delivery mechanisms, cultures, and tastes that are readily available today.

This kind of divergence or specialisation has taken place across industries. From health clubs that used to offer only weights, to the plethora of fitness classes offered today such as Yoga, Barre, Zumba, Pilates, spinning—to technology-enabled fitness that beams a spinning class from a studio in NYC right to your bike in the comfort of your own home, as offered by the Peloton bike.

Even email has diverged. First, there was only email, which you used to send business messages, make plans, share jokes, share photos, wish people birthdays, and so on. Now for rapid communication with people you know well there is WhatsApp for acquaintances, text or SMS, Facebook for birthdays, Instagram and Snapchat for photos, Slack for internal teams, and so forth.

It's fun to take a look at a product or service offering that is readily available today and track it back in its path of evolution and see where it all started.

Aside from being a fun exercise of trying to look at where a product or service emerged having travelled on the divergence path, the reason this concept of divergence is important is because this law of nature gives us a very effective strategy of understanding an important accelerator of success: **specialisation.**

If you want to become a super successful salesperson or move faster up the corporate ladder, it is critical that you gain visibility. Customers, colleagues, and managers need to see and notice you. And it becomes difficult to do that if you're one of a hundred marketing people. But you're more likely to find luck getting noticed if you're one in a department of five or six people. Let me share with you how I accelerated my career at one of the biggest companies in the world by working in a department of six people.

Finding My Niche in Corporate America – Bob

After a few years of success as a #1 sales representative for Pfizer with my sales territory in New York City, I was able to move to a job in the company's global world headquarters on 42nd Street in New York in a small unknown department called International Pricing Administration.

I landed the job through a series of incidental meetings. I have talked about these in my motivational videos which are on YouTube.

Quite early in my career—when I didn't know much about pricing after I moved from being a sales rep to the corporate office—I had a good manager who helped me transition from the field to a corporate environment and trained me. As a junior manager in the pricing department, my job was to help Pfizer's country operations to obtain approval from senior Pfizer management on pricing for new product launches, changes to pricing across the portfolio of products, and also to maintain a database of prices for all the products around the world.

It wasn't the ideal job I had imagined when I was out pounding the pavement as a rep but I was grateful for the chance to move up into corporate headquarters. At the time, the entire pricing department was made up of six people, which included two administrative assistants. Our offices were located on the floor of a worn down old building that Pfizer had leased for its back-office operations. Our group had no visibility, no budget and initially, it didn't appear as a path up the career ladder. It was thought of as the place where employees were sent to slowly fade until they retired. The group leader was very close to retirement. It was a no man's land.

I was still enthusiastic because coming from the sales force, I naively saw the job as a stepping stone to better and bigger things. Like in many big companies at the time, the marketing department was where the real action was, given that the company was launching new products almost every year. Most of the senior management came through the marketing division and if I ever wanted to move up, I was advised by senior colleagues that I would need to have marketing experience.

After a couple of years in the pricing department, I decided to apply for a job in marketing because I felt that being in pricing wasn't going to lead anywhere. I was doing mundane tasks such as maintaining a database and ensuring appropriate controls for management on the paperwork. I felt more like a bureaucrat than a professional manager. I wasn't making any impact. Nothing I did truly made a difference to the growth or success of the company. I was in an administrative job when I thought I should have a marketing job, which was more in line with the business. So, I did what most of us would do. I applied for a job out of there!

At the time, Pfizer was just starting to be known as a marketing powerhouse run by a charismatic head of marketing. Gracing the covers of marketing magazines and trade journals, this person was the quintessential marketing guy who took pride in hiring all the marketing and brand managers himself and pouring his life into the job. He created the Pfizer softball league consisting mainly of hundred or so marketing managers in Pfizer's corporate office on 42nd St.

Marketing was the place to be if you were going to rise and succeed at Pfizer and getting into a role there, was more difficult than I expected. It was a closed and almost tribe-like culture where it seemed that you had to have an MBA from a top University, had to love baseball and be able to talk the bold lingo of aggressive marketers in order to get in.

And while I had been a successful sales star, the hiring manager of the marketing job I had applied for didn't see me as great potential for a marketing star at Pfizer. So, I got rejected. And in those years once you got rejected from one job in marketing, it was difficult to even apply for other jobs in marketing.

Feeling deflated, I got depressed at my bad luck. I blamed my lack of an MBA degree from a top school and not being into baseball or fitting into the corporate culture in marketing, at Pfizer.

After some time wallowing in the disappointment and being down, I decided to get back to work in my tiny cubicle and threw myself into the job. I became recommitted and started to focus inward. It wasn't because I thought pricing was going to be my ticket to success. I decided to refocus on pricing because I needed to take my mind off from the negativity I was feeling.

Looking back, getting rejected by the marketing department was the best thing that ever happened to me because it forced me to pursue unchartered waters.

Doing my job with greater intensity and focus was refreshing because it allowed me to escape negative thinking from the rejection that I had thought stopped my growth.

Have you ever felt like you were stuck in a job that was going nowhere? You're really smart but no one is giving you a chance?

As I began working longer hours to keep away the thoughts of a stymied career, I started learning about how pricing was done in countries around the world. I learned about the detailed and complex structures governments had set up for their countries. How governments viewed healthcare and insurance, how they negotiated pricing with pharmaceutical companies, what sort of rules they had set up to determine reimbursement for pharmaceutical products, and much more.

I became more curious.

My curiosity led me to notice something interesting. I began to observe an interesting trend. I started noticing that our department was getting more frequent requests for price reductions from our country operations in Europe. As Pfizer's country operations needed to seek permission for price changes, they would have to submit a standardised form to our department which we would then send to senior management for their approval. Operations in France, Italy, and Spain among others were being forced by their respective governments to reduce prices more frequently and earlier in the year.

This observation led me to a simple question: Why?

Why were these countries trying to reduce prices? Or more specifically why were the governments in these countries forcing pharmaceutical companies, including Pfizer to reduce prices? What was going on here?

That question intrigued me and thus began my journey deeper into unchartered waters. At the time in 1996, the Internet was still at a nascent stage so there wasn't much information available online. A few books were written on the subject that were really not very useful. So, I did what I loved to do: call people. I called my Pfizer colleagues across Europe and began a search to learn and understand what was going on. My own deep dive into learning led me to speak to almost a hundred colleagues spread out through various divisions and management levels. I was curious about what was happening on the ground and the closest I could get to the ground were my colleagues who were living and working in these countries.

Spreading my net of learning far and wide, I started to attend little known seminars around the subject of pricing which were attended by only a dozen or so people in those days. Not content with simply sitting and listening to the speakers, I chased after them after their talks and threw a barrage of questions at them.

I was becoming passionately interested in a field that was yet undeveloped. I didn't know at the time it but I was becoming an expert in healthcare systems around the world, particularly on pricing.

As a result of my speaking to hundreds of people learning about what was happening and why prices were changing so frequently, I got this understanding that fundamentally, the pharmaceutical industry was headed for significant disruption.

Governments were running out of money at the beginning of the year to spend on pharmaceuticals for their citizens. Unlike the US, European governments pay for and subsidise all of healthcare for their populations. As such, they are in a sense the buyers of pharmaceuticals. They're the payers. And given that so many pharmaceutical companies were launching new drugs almost every other month in the late 1990s, the government's costs were rising and thus causing a strain on their drug budget earlier and earlier each year. They were running out of money so they were forcing pharmaceutical companies to change prices.

In 1997, this was an incredibly unique insight and no one else had this level of detailed knowledge about it. No one was capturing this emerging trend in the company. Sure, there were those in some countries that were seeing it from their local perspective but not as a whole. But I could see it from my tiny cubicle in the corporate office in NYC. Today, this seems obvious but at the time, this was a huge revelation.

Chance Favours the Expert

As the months passed, I got a deeper understanding into the problem from several different angles. This 360-degree perspective also gave me clues to what a solution might look like. To help me think through an approach of how we might deal with this imminent big problem of payers not willing to pay for our products, I started writing up my learnings in a concept paper.

Then almost suddenly something interesting happened. Pricing became important to the company. And especially to the top management of the company.

Governments continued to put pressure on the company's business more frequently and senior management, who essentially came from the world of marketing weren't sure how to handle it. One senior leader in the company, in particular, was keen on gaining a richer understanding of the scope of the problem and what, if anything, could be done about it.

Because this was such a small, narrow field of interest, when that senior leader of the company wanted to talk to someone to understand the issue, there were only two people he could talk to. And I happened to be one of them and ultimately became his most trusted advisor on the topic.

Since I was an expert in this field, I started being invited to important senior management meetings even though I was a very junior person in the company. I took on high-level projects and initiatives in the area of pricing that started to spread the knowledge of my learnings to the rest of the company. As more and more issues around pricing emerged, I started to help senior people deal with these problems thoughtfully.

As I began realising that the company needed to do more around this area in late 1999, I turned my concept paper with all my learnings into a bold proposal to create a whole new function in the company that would be dedicated to working with governments around pricing and reimbursement. I pitched the idea to one of Pfizer's senior business leaders, suggesting that the company should create the Market Access function.

My proposal took a year to get off the ground but eventually, it did. I was given the green light. And as a result, I got appointed as the first person in the company to lead the development of the function in the entire company and got tasked with the job of creating a similar role of Market Access in each of Pfizer's operations around the world, starting with Europe. Today, this function is one of the most important capabilities in a pharmaceutical company and employs thousands of people worldwide, working with governments on pricing, reimbursement, and value. While marketing is still important in most pharmaceutical companies, it does not hold as much weight as the market access function.

From the moment I got appointed into the new role, my career trajectory accelerated. I got promoted, was given more team members to manage and bigger budgets to handle. Most importantly, I started adding significant value to the company and helping people in the company learn and understand the world of pricing and reimbursement.

I was in the right place at the right time—with the right expertise. I got lucky.

By chance, I created my own luck by finding a niche in a field where no one was playing in and focusing really deep on learning, understanding, and becoming an expert. It wasn't easy to do because I saw everyone else go into marketing and grow and get promoted from product launch to product launch. I wasn't one of hundreds at a marketing conference. I was one of six at a pricing conference. And at times it felt uneasy because I wasn't sure if I was on the right track since no one else had been on that track before me. But I persisted on following that track because of a combination of curiosity and belief.

I observed something new and asked "why?"

I was able to radically grow my career in one of the biggest companies in the world by using the same principle that Rehan used to make his startup, Flora2000, a success. The principle of divergence. It led me to go in the opposite direction of where everyone else was focused. I found a narrow field without competitors and pursued it and became an expert who was sought out for his expertise.

Luck Byte

Find an unexplored area and go deep. Learn, understand, get a granular, laser-like focus on a specific field and become a master. At the smallest and narrowest part of your industry. Once you do, you'll notice people asking you for advice, thoughts, and ideas. You will start receiving invitations to present and share your knowledge. You'll receive valuable job offers. You'll increase your chances of luck appearing in your startup, your career, and your life.

Key Learnings

1. In the beginning, avoid the temptation to go after a large market. Don't compete in a large crowded market because it takes far more resources and energy to get noticed. Choose a smaller, more niche area where you have a higher chance of being visible to those that matter.

2. Specialise. By going deeper into a very narrow field, you have a better chance at creating breakthrough experiences for those you are trying to impress. Narrow doesn't mean less—it means more. More in-depth knowledge about the needs and desires and the problem—all of which help the customer or your managers realise that you know them really well.

3. Don't do things better. Do them differently. Create a better experience for customers. Find a way that stands out of the crowd.

My Action Plan

1. **What is the narrow field where I know I can dominate?**

   ....
   ....
   ....
   ....

2. **What am I doing to specialise and get really deep into understanding my marketplace or field or area?**

   ....
   ....
   ....
   ....

3. **What is the one thing I need to do less of to get laser-focused on being seen as an expert or really knowledgeable by those who matter? What can I do to demonstrate to my customers that I really know what I am talking about?**

   ....
   ....
   ....
   ....

Luck byte

*Visualise the result of your goals so clearly that
the image pulls you toward it every day.*

CHAPTER 4

HAVE A BEGINNER'S MINDSET. LISTEN TO THE CRITICS. BE OPEN MINDED

In Zen Buddhism, there is a very powerful word for helping people achieve great success in any endeavour. This word encompasses a principle used by the world's most accomplished people from super successful entrepreneurs to salespeople and business leaders alike. The word is:

Shoshin.

The translation of *Shoshin* is quite simple but has a profound impact on your ability to boost success.

It means "beginner's mind".

It is referred to as "having an attitude of openness, eagerness, and lack of preconceptions in the study of a subject even when studying at an advanced level, just as a beginner in that subject would." The famous Zen teacher, Shunryu Suzuki said correctly,

"In the beginner's mind, there are many possibilities, in the expert's mind, there are few."

Armed with strong and deep knowledge of our chosen field of endeavour, sometimes it's easy to think that we know it all. That we have years of experience, connections, and a deep understanding of our marketplace that can serve us as we face obstacles and decisions. The problem with having such deep expertise is that it can often blind us to realising great success.

This is because when you face challenges, you tend to ignore ideas given that you don't like where they came from. You make the mistake of judging the person's ability or knowledge before you accept the idea. Just because someone may not know as much as you do about your industry, you close your mind.

According to researchers, self-proclaimed experts can be closed-minded. In a 2015 study[*] published in the *Journal of Experimental Social Psychology*, researchers found that the smarter you think you are, the more you are likely to conform

---

[*]   Ottatia, Victor, Erika D. Price, Chase Wilson, and Nathanael Sumaktoyob. "When self-perceptions of expertise increase closed-minded cognition: The earned dogmatism effect" *Journal of Experimental Social Psychology*, Volume 61, November 2015: 131-138 https://www.sciencedirect.com/science/article/pii/S002210311 5001006

to ideas that support your personal biases. And by sticking to your own views you reduce your ability to get new ideas or novel approaches to solving problems and generating the level of improvement you might need to grow your business or career.

When you're working to grow a business or your career, you will encounter many challenges.

Why isn't anyone buying my product?

How come our business is not growing when we're throwing everything at it?

How can I hire good people when I don't have enough to pay them?

How can I get promoted and earn more money in my career?

How can I get recognised in the marketplace?

Are the terms of this fundraising good for my business?

And so on. Most questions won't be as easy as those mentioned above. And so, it is very important to have an open mind because it allows you to be more aware of ideas to solve some of the toughest problems you're going to face.

Here's how.

Listen.

Understand.

Fight the urge to reject criticism or objections.

Ask yourself: "What am I missing here?"

Think through your problem. Focus on what was said, not who said it. Control the ego.

And then ASK others for their advice, opinion, and insight.

Ask them with the beginner's mind: "What am I missing here?" "Am I being too blinded by my personal bias?"

You cannot build a successful business or career alone.

You need the advice, guidance, support, and instruction from a diverse pool of people around you. Whether you get a coach, a mentor, a board member, or a friend, you need to proactively reach out to a strong and valuable network of people who don't necessarily think like you do.

In fact, it's better if they don't agree with you most of the time because that's how you'll build a stronger business. That's how you'll accelerate your career. Because these people will show you your blind spots. They'll be able to honestly share why they think you're wrong. And it will make you think about how to address the problems they've raised, helping you improve your product offering or your skill set.

If you listen and try to understand, you're more likely to improve your chance of making a breakthrough change in your career or company

But you've got to **listen**. You've got to understand. Take those insights and get the mind's engine working.

We believe that in the vigorous pursuit of success in your field, you must have an open mind that embraces difficult objections, listens to unappealing criticisms, and most of all forces you to be aware of your own failings.

Having an open mind in times of problems, criticisms, and objections is important because it helps us become better at what we're trying to achieve. This is especially true for those building a startup business because there are so many obstacles, critics, and challenges that come your way that the only way to overcome them is to address them head-on. And use those criticisms to fuel your growth forward.

Country Delight & GoMechanic – Rehan

There is a basic human desire that often limits our chances to rapidly grow a business. And that is the need to be consistent. We like to be consistent with what we believed in the past, who we were while growing up, and our view of our product or service at the time we started our company. We want to be consistent with who we might have been or believed yesterday.

While this is a valuable trait in how we deal fairly in our relationships with other people and remain true to our core selves, in the world of startups and business it can hold back our growth. Often referred to as founder's myopia, our desire to hold on to the view of our original idea of our product or service as we want it to be can be detrimental. Founders who can break out of the founder's myopia and see a broader, bigger world, and make it less about them and more about adapting to the changing needs of the marketplace can greatly accelerate their startups to huge success.

Country Delight

Milk is one of the oldest products in India and has changed little since the revolution in the 1970s. Millions love milk and get their share delivered each morning. Founders Chakradhar Gade and Nitin Kaushal of the startup Country Delight launched a company to change the way people consume milk. Around 2015, they had the insight that Indian households wanted fresh and pure milk because consumers were dissatisfied with the milk they were getting from state co-operatives such as Amul, Vijaya, Nandini, and others, which was often reconstituted from milk powder and treated at ultra-high temperatures, making it essentially a 'dead' product.

Country Delight wanted to bring fresh milk to consumers directly and so, they started selling milk as a premium offering from single origin farms in beautiful glass bottle packaging that was double the price of the milk being offered by the state co-operatives. While this strategy got them noticed in the marketplace because it was a new way to think about a very old product, it didn't make a significant impact on their business. Their business started off doing well but they weren't breaking through in a big way. Luck did not favour them for a couple of years.

Feedback from critics, friends, advisors, and customers showed that the price was just too high compared to their competition. This got the founders thinking about:

- How can we lower our price to that level? There would be no margins.
- How can we say we are this beautifully crafted product if we lower our price?
- How will we appear in the marketplace when we go back on what we believed in?

- Don't we believe in our premium product?
- What are we missing here?

After many difficult conversations, the founders decided to let go of their previous way of thinking and adjusted to the voices of the market. They decided to use the beginners mind to rethink their entire business, not just price but the entire back end supply chain, packaging, and more. This was hard to do not because it was a difficult road to climb with uncertainty on the horizon but because our human desire of not wanting to be seen as inconsistent. These founders wanted to be consistent with what they launched because that's what drove them to create the business in the first place. And now, to abandon that idea and succumb to a lower price was a difficult choice. I believe they ultimately realised that in order to grow considerably, they had to be open-minded and listen to the critics and advisors. And not let the past hold them back from growing in the future.

I think that's really the key here – to recognise that what got you here is not what's going to get you there – where success is, ultimately. And to leave behind the ideas of yesterday and embrace the ideas that the market is asking for.

Once that decision was made, the founders recreated their entire model. They developed a revision of their supply chain, packaging, and distribution chain. They moved away from single farms; instead, they started using high quality testing equipment to ascertain quality from multiple farms. They changed the packaging from a glass bottle, which was expensive, to a simple plastic pouch. And they started using gig economy workers to deliver the product.

This took time but more importantly, it took commitment to be open to everything and anything. As a result, their business started to grow and flourish and has been growing at 5x a year, attracting investment from major VCs, greatly increasing their valuation. But more importantly, by embracing the situation with an open mind, they were able to reach more customers in more places than ever.

GoMechanic

Another example is that of GoMechanic, a startup founded by Amit Bhasin and Kushal Karwa. Their insight was that car owners can either fix and service their car at an authorised service center or at a local garage and there seemed to be dissatisfaction at both ends. Car owners received large bills from authorised service centers or poor service and a lower bill from local garages.

Their innovative solution was to convert local garages into GoMechanic garages by providing them branding, training, and standard operating procedures, along with computerisation. This worked well for a while as car owners began to take notice of their consumer ads and publicity. However, they weren't growing. The idea to go after more of a business-to-business (B2B) market was discussed and initially dismissed because profit margins weren't as lucrative as in the consumer market.

They saw themselves as a consumer-focused business

in their initial launch. Once you see yourself as something specific, it's hard to change because again, human beings like to be consistent. But after some time, they realised that to grow on a massive scale, they needed to think differently – to use the beginner's mind.

Onboarding the right garages was key. But how to do it? They had to rethink the focus away from consumers to B2B and go after fleet operators. The idea was: if they had the demand with cars, it would attract garages to sign up faster. Even with lower margins, servicing a fleet of cars would give them the volume they needed to convince local garages to rebrand under the GoMechanic umbrella.

By adopting the beginner's mind, they broke out of the trap of founder's myopia and were able to change with where the market was going. More and more cars were on ride-sharing platforms such as Ola and Uber. And so, they changed their business model to first go after the volume offered by partnerships with fleet operators such as Uber by being their preferred garage partner in any major city. After they built the base with fleet owners and garages, they started to go after consumer business again. This pivot resulted in massive volume growth to GoMechanic's business, resulting in 10x growth in 2018-2019.

Entrepreneurs often put brakes on their success by thinking they know so much. Successful entrepreneurs recognise that they have yet to scratch the surface of knowledge and insight and so, force themselves to always keep an open mind. No one can be sure about which ideas will work and which won't. That's why it's important not to place judgement on any ideas. Instead, try to encourage bringing out these ideas from others.

Always be proactive about how you incorporate the beginner's mind in helping generate ideas and solutions for your business. Create a board that will really challenge you and is not afraid to disagree with you. Have a number of friends and advisors around you who think differently than you do. Look to peer mentorship networks that can give you advice and direction.

Having a vibrant and diverse group of peers and mentors is important but the most important thing to do is to be mindful enough to ask them: "What am I missing?"

Using Criticism to Fuel Growth – Bob

After I had left my long career at Pfizer, I decided to take a big risk and join a small startup that had this incredibly powerful technology using manufactured DNA to track products in the supply chain. The company invited me to join because I was a pharmaceutical industry expert and they were looking for someone senior to take it to pharma.

After joining them I spent months studying and learning about the technology, the marketplace, the problems, and the obstacles as well as the competing technologies, which looked very weak and vulnerable compared to our technology. I spent countless hours researching the competing product and trying to break it apart so that I could find our product's USP—Unique Selling Proposition—to make it look superior to our customers and prospects.

After a few short months of generating confidence in our product, I began to go out into the market and started pitching pharmaceutical companies. In one sales pitch with a large US pharma company, my colleague Tom and I were presenting to a group of about ten people and somewhere towards the middle of our meeting, I realised that the audience was turning, and not in a good way. In the beginning, they were keen to learn and understand our technology. But as we got farther along in our pitch and the more confidence we showed, the more they tore apart our arguments.

The people in the room loved using this one particular competing product and they used it all the time. And they saw no need for a product like ours in the marketplace. Zero. The confidence that we displayed initially in our product burst like a balloon dashing any hopes of a second meeting with the prospect.

I went home that day, feeling deflated and to make myself feel better, told myself that these guys were backward. They had no clue as to what they were doing using that old competing product. What did they know?!?! I was the one here passionate about this new breakthrough technology and they were the ones using the old crude system that wasn't going to do anything for them. I had worked in pharma for twenty-three years and knew as much if not more than they did.

For months, I dismissed the criticism we received from those potential customers. I looked at them as a group of people who didn't have the appreciation for great technology such as ours. I ignored the critics.

But as time passed, I started to hear some similar

arguments in other potential customers. And with a sense of frustration, I began asking myself "What am I missing here? What did they tell us that I didn't get?"

That was the key. I asked myself the question. It wasn't self-doubt that caused me to reconsider their opinion but rather a sense of curiosity as to why they would reject our product for this old competing product.

This is important. When we come at the criticism with a sense of hurt, we have a tough time learning from it and growing from it. Instead, we need to come at criticism with a beginner's mind, which places no emotion and no judgement on to it—and only looks at it from the viewpoint of learning and understanding.

And so now with the ego put aside, I was able to think about that question with a beginner's mind. With no attachment or judgement. Once I detached any feeling of emotion from my intention to understand, the answer came to me only a few short weeks later.

I realised that I was going about my marketing and sales pitch completely the wrong way. The competing product they were using was good. In fact, it was excellent. And they should continue to use it. But the breakthrough realisation was that our product wouldn't necessarily replace the competing product but be used in a completely different way. In fact, the competition was not really competition!

This thread of understanding helped me think about a completely new and exciting way to position my product to customers that gave us the edge we needed to get into the market.

As a result, our value proposition improved tremendously

and along with it a renewed sense of confidence. After this breakthrough when we approached potential customers with a more thoughtful and reasonable approach, we started to get more traction and with it more success.

That success only came when I put aside my ego and proactively looked at the criticism as an opportunity to learn. I had no idea that there were jewels of opportunity hidden in the critics' voices—opportunities to make my product better, opportunities to make myself better.

Key Learnings

1. Don't ignore the critics. Embrace them. There are jewels hidden inside of their criticism. Find a way to learn from them and what they say. Use their voices to improve and grow.
2. Have the mindset of a student, of a beginner, of a novice. Place no judgement or emotion on what people say. Only learn from it.
3. Create a wide and deep network of friends, peers, mentors, and advisors. Invite people who think differently than you to be part of your mentor circle. Force your circle to ask you tough questions that you may not like. Only by thinking hard and answering their questions can you grow exponentially.

My Action Plan

1. **What do the critics say about you or your product or company that you don't like? Is there something**

you can learn from them? What is the jewel hidden underneath the criticism?

....
....
....
....

2. What I am doing every day to keep a beginner's mind?

....
....
....
....

3. Name five people who don't agree with you or think like you. Commit to calling these people frequently and asking them for advice or ideas or insight.

....
....
....
....
....

Luck byte

Make one new friend a week and your network will blossom exponentially.

CHAPTER 5

DO WHAT IS HARD

**"A smooth sea never made
a skilled sailor"**

We face choices each day. Some are easy. Some are hard. Some seem doable. Some seem impossible and require a lot of hard work, tremendous effort, and seem a long way off. None guarantee that we'll be successful.

Most of us don't wish to face pain and don't like suffering. In fact, we have a natural tendency to avoid things that are uncomfortable, difficult, and painful. From tough conversations to difficult decisions, we don't like to make them, put them off, and often go to great lengths to avoid them altogether.

We have come to the realisation that to accelerate and push the boundaries of success in today's super competitive business environment, we must invite discomfort and endure some level of suffering to achieve greatness in our startup, in our career, and in our lives.

When faced with a choice, we must pick the hard choice.

We must choose the hard path.

We must do what is difficult.

We must always select the hard path.

Why?

First, it is because the hard path is more likely to give you growth than the easy path.

"The mind is a muscle and requires tension and resistance to grow. If you want to grow, you must take the hard path."
-Bob Miglani

When you walk on the hard path, you are more likely to encounter problems and challenges. And learning how to face these challenges will make you stronger, better, and more effective. Facing these challenges will force you to either quit or to figure out ways to overcome them, raising your level of creativity, and forcing you to build your skills and resources to meet these challenges.

Most people think that successful people don't have any problems. That's 100% wrong. Super successful people have plenty of problems. In fact, successful people are more likely to encounter problems because they are out there trying to build bold and super successful businesses and lives. Their secret is not that they avoid problems or buy themselves out of it. The real secret to their success is that they have learned how to handle problems. That's the true secret to success—to be able to handle problems with creativity, skill, calm, and with an open mind.

And learning to do so will leapfrog your way to success. And the only way you can learn is by pursuing the hard path.

Second, the hard path is less likely to be followed by your competitors. Whether you are competing with hundreds of sales reps for a coveted prize or trying to raise funds for your startup, if you take the hard path, your competitors will have a difficult time copying you or taking away business from you.

When you do what is hard, you will in effect be creating a moat—an impenetrable wall that your competitors will find difficult to climb.

Sure, there are variations of easy and hard paths. However, when we boil it down to the fundamental truth, **we often know the right path** to take, yet we struggle with making a decision or a choice because the **path we must take is often a gruelling one fraught with obstacles, unknowns, and hard work.** Back-breaking, gut-wrenching work—and a lot of it.

Whether we're trying to build a new business or make a major career shift choosing the hard path is not our first choice.

Why Should We Intentionally Pursue the Hard Path?

Because the hard path is often the one that we must be on but the fear of failure keeps us from making this choice.

We are afraid that we won't make it. We are afraid of the "not enough" problem...

- Not enough money
- Not enough knowledge
- Not enough courage
- Not enough strength
- Not enough time
- Not enough energy
- Not enough experience
- Not enough skill
- Not good enough
- Not enough this or that

But the Hard Path Is Worth It

We have to do what's hard in life because that is often what is needed.

We have to choose the hard path because that is what **will mould us into the person we are meant to become.**

We must choose the hard path because that is what **will dramatically change the trajectory of our business.**

We need to choose the hard path because that **will alter the course of our future.**

The hard path is where we get the optimum growth, meet the best people, learn things we never could have imagined, feel every emotion and become better, stronger and more successful.

Hard Versus Easy

To truly transform ourselves, we must do what is hard. But it's not an easy decision to make. It requires us to give up our time, money, effort, and energy. We will have to make major sacrifices.

> **"If you want the life others don't have,**
> **you have to be willing**
> **to do what others don't do."**
> **-Les Brown**

The Hard Path Creates a Moat – Rehan

When I had launched my startup Flora2000 and it wasn't doing well, I had discovered that there might be potential for this whole new market for US-based Indians who wanted to send flowers to their loved ones in India. Similarly, there might be customers who wanted to send flowers to Germany, Brazil, Japan, and many countries around the world.

This was immensely complex and a logistics nightmare. I would have to figure out time zones, local addresses, holidays, distribution patterns, delivery options from one country to another, and currencies—all while trying to maintain the quality of fresh flowers that would die if not handled in the right conditions.

It was an agonising decision I had to make to move Flora2000 away from an e-commerce floral delivery for India to a floral delivery for US customers who wanted to send flowers all over the world. It was a more difficult choice but I chose it because I saw no other option to make my startup successful. I chose the hard path.

And that hard path made all the difference in the world. **It is because a hard path is also one that is very difficult to follow or copy.** Most other people won't do what's hard. We were able to become successful and stay successful for so long precisely because we are able to persevere and solve the complex problems of logistics, delivery, freshness, time zones, and several other issues while our competitors didn't even bother to do it. Some of our competitors tried but gave up.

What this did was to create a moat around our castle to protect us from the competition.

Today, there are a number of examples of startups who are taking the hard path and those who are not.

Take for example Zomato, the restaurant delivery startup that launched some years ago. They aggregate restaurants on their app and help consumers get delivery of food from the restaurant. They were very successful when they launched and had almost a 90% market share.

But the problem with food delivery in India is that it is inconsistent and fraught with poor service and very difficult to have seamless high-quality delivery from the restaurants.

Zomato did something that was not easy to do but it wasn't that difficult either. They aggregated restaurants for the consumer. But in this hyper-competitive world, it wasn't enough.

Along came Swiggy, a similar food delivery startup that did something hard. They delivered the food from the restaurant <u>themselves</u>. They hired delivery staff to deliver the food from the restaurant to the consumer directly on motorbikes. From handling logistics to hiring and training drivers to figuring out routes and efficient driving patterns, Swiggy did what was hard. All for enhancing and improving the customer experience.

As a result, Swiggy is surpassing Zomato by leaps. Today, Swiggy has over 100,000 drivers across the markets they are in. Customers see a Swiggy driver with food from their favourite restaurant and get it in a consistent, convenient manner. As an investor, while I missed out on the opportunity to invest in Swiggy, I admire their desire to do something that was hard. They don't just aggregate—they deliver. They followed the hard path of hiring delivery staff because they wanted to do something different that the customer wanted. In the end, it will be difficult to tell who or which startup will win out over the longer term but what is clear is that a startup needs to take the difficult route because the competitors are out there waiting and most likely willing to do what it takes to succeed.

The Moat Makes the Difference
– Rehan & Bob

moat
mōt/
noun
1. a deep, wide ditch surrounding a castle, fort, or town, typically filled with water and intended as a defense against attack.

PharmEasy is a startup my fund, Orios, has invested in and is an excellent example of following this key principle of success—of doing what is hard. Initially, like many startups, they started out aggregating retailers—in their case, chemists and neighbourhood pharmacies through their app. A consumer goes on the PharmEasy app and scans their prescription for the medicine and PharmEasy relays the prescription to the most convenient pharmacy store. The pharmacy then delivers the medicine to the patient.

The problem that Dr Dhaval Shah and Dharmil Sheth, PharmEasy Co-Founders, faced with this model was similar to that of Zomato's. It was relatively easy for consumers to use and also easy to copy the aggregation model. Soon enough it would face enormous competition. Tying up with pharmacies and asking them to deliver was easy to do. But in the hot and competitive startup climate that we live in today, it's also very easy to fail, doing what everyone else does.

As Dhaval explains, their rationale was to have a hard look at their business and go full force to pursue a very different path—one that is hard.

First, the customer experience was terrible. Delivery from the pharmacy to the consumer was awful. Sometimes the delivery person picked up the wrong medication or it was not stored at proper temperatures. Drivers from the pharmacy spoke poorly and sometimes behaved badly with customers. They weren't on time and made a lot of errors, resulting in having to return products and the customer dropping the service altogether.

Second, 70% of the orders were initially rejected because patients didn't have a valid prescription from their doctor. This is common in India.

Third, there were about twenty-five competitors in India trying to do the same thing—get into the medicine delivery business.

So, Dhaval and Dharmil decided to take the hard path. Here's what they did.

They decided that their startup had to focus on three very important facets for creating a super successful business.

1. Create a superb customer experience.
2. Create value for everyone in the entire ecosystem of healthcare.
3. Build a moat around their system so others would have a difficult time copying them.

Specifically, they handled each of their challenges as follows:

First, PharmEasy created a platform for those patients who did not have a valid prescription to have an online conversation with a doctor so that they could get one. This was unheard of and difficult to pull off. Since patients were not used to having a prescription from a doctor, PharmEasy had to educate each patient. Also, PharmEasy had to create a whole new product and platform for recruiting and retaining doctors who would be willing to talk to patients online and be able to give them a valid prescription. In itself, setting up such a doctor to patient platform is a company and business on its own.

Second, PharmEasy decided to take on the last leg of the delivery on their own. To help the end consumer get the best customer experience, they started hiring and training drivers on motorbikes to deliver the medicine from the pharmacy directly to the customer. This boosted trust, reliability, and customer experience.

Third, in addition to procuring the medicines from local pharmacies, PharmEasy decided to go right up to the distributor and eventually to the manufacturers themselves. Buying the product directly from the manufacturer allows the company to have more control over the entire pharmaceutical supply chain so as to provide better margins, better service, and delivery.

All of these strategies that PharmEasy deployed were really hard to do. They could have built a nice business around just being a pharmacy aggregator. They could have built a deeper network of pharmacies and helped them do better delivery themselves. They could have simply gone around the fact that most people don't have prescriptions from the doctor. They could have done all those things and maybe they would have been successful. In fact, just on that alone, they were able to raise a lot of money.

But no. They didn't do what is easy. They did something that was hard. Hiring and training a fleet of delivery vehicles is expensive and time consuming with logistical challenges every step of the way. Developing arrangements with doctors is filled with roadblocks and obstacles. And then getting into the wholesale distribution business—with large warehouses, delivery trucks, operational software, and then delivery on top of that.

As a result of choosing the hard path, Dhaval and his co-founder have put the company on the path of success because they have built a moat around their entire business. Think about how difficult it will be for a competitor to start a fleet of delivery vehicles. Or how the complexity of setting up a doctor-patient platform will scare away those who are trying to copy their model.

> **"When you do something hard, it is difficult for most people to follow and replace you."**
> **-Bob Miglani**

PharmEasy is growing faster than ever and taking on hundreds of new customers each day putting them on a remarkable and accelerated path of success. At the time of the publishing this book, it is the market leader in E-Pharmacy in India.

> **"Do what is easy and your life will be hard.**
> **Do what is hard and your life will be easy."**
> **-Les Brown**

Ola Leasing

Initially, Ola Cabs started as an aggregation model but soon discovered that they ran out of cars across India. There weren't enough cars for the supply of drivers who wanted to drive. And the demand was growing exponentially. So, they did something hard. Ola Leasing was born. Instead of sticking to the aggregation model alone, they took on the challenge of creating a supply of cars for drivers to lease. Today, Ola Cabs owns the largest fleet of cars in India, which they rent to drivers on a daily basis. This is a big moat, as it makes vehicles available exclusively to those who want to drive for Ola. The additional payoff is that this business, which is housed in a subsidiary, is highly profitable and something Ola can IPO in its own right.

Everything is an academic exercise until it impacts your own life – Bob

Investing in a hard strategy is a monumentally difficult decision as the founder of a startup. You're betting on a path which takes a lot more time to execute with more unpredictable variables that could potentially lead to a big failure.

But I would wager that taking the hard path when it

comes to a decision that impacts your life and that of your family's is even more difficult to make. And one that has the possibility of bringing with it not only massive risk but also massive success and luck.

You invest a million dollars in a hard path marketing strategy and you lose it all. It might jeopardize your startup in that moment. But you could also raise more money.

Leave a good job with a hugely successful company and choose to do something unproven? Well, that's excruciatingly hard.

But I believe that that's exactly what we have to do today if we're to increase the odds of luck coming into our work, our career, and our life. And I base this on a core principle I believe in, which is this: <u>The mind is a muscle and requires resistance and tension for it to grow. If we want to grow our mind and in turn grow our life, we have to do what is hard.</u> We must encounter resistance. We have to choose the life where there are challenges and obstacles because that path is where we will find our greatest strengths and develop incredible skills, and see them unveiling themselves in front of our very eyes.

After twenty-three years of working at Pfizer, I was in a good job, in a big, hugely successful company. Yes, there were challenges every day in the business in the marketplace and in my role. But by and large, it was a good path. It wasn't easy but it wasn't hard either. Showing up at the office, working hard, contributing, being flexible and adapting to the changes, working with colleagues, dealing with the challenges and then going home. It was a relatively safe environment.

I had a good job but I wasn't growing. Sure, there were opportunities for different roles within the company going after new markets, new geographies, managing bigger budgets, or larger teams but I still felt constricted.

With so much change happening in the world from the growth of technology to demographic shifts to the way we work and live—everything was changing outside. But inside, working at Pfizer, I realised that I wasn't changing as fast I wanted to. I wasn't growing.

A friend outside Pfizer invited me to his office one day where he was hosting the CEO of a small company who was giving a talk about new technologies and tools for research and development in the pharmaceutical industry. Upon listening to his presentation, I sat in amazement at some of the cutting-edge things that were taking place in this tiny little company that was completely unknown. I walked out of that introductory session thinking how amazing it was to have such innovative work being done not by a huge company like Pfizer but a small three-person outfit in the middle of nowhere. Imagine how many other companies were out there in the world just like this one, I thought to myself. As I continued walking back to my office at Pfizer that day, I asked myself if I was losing my edge. How could I not be aware of such massive advances in the way R&D was being done in my industry? Was doing the same-old-same-old in my job holding back my learning and growth? Was I getting too comfortable in my job? What else was I missing? Why wasn't I getting involved in such exciting growth opportunities? Why wasn't I sharp as I used to be? Was I getting complacent?

Maybe it was because my company was at a stage where there was less creative room for executives. Or maybe I had simply been there too long. Or I was in the wrong division of the company. Whatever the case, I felt that the world was changing at such a rapid pace that maybe I needed to change too.

But change to what?

I was making good money and financially it didn't make sense to leave. It wasn't practical. With a lucrative compensation package, a healthy savings plan, good health insurance, and stock options, I had too good a job to leave and no idea exactly what I was going to do afterwards. Where would I make the kind of money that I was so accustomed to receiving from working at Pfizer? My speaking career was going well but as I was working full time at Pfizer, it became limited.

The world outside the window from my corporate office on 42nd street looked hard.

I looked around at those who were a few years senior to me and some who were in their fifties having a difficult time in their careers within the company. Their jobs were changing and they felt threatened that they might not make it through the next round of organisational changes and cuts. They were still a few years away from being eligible for the retirement benefits that were typically given in big companies like Pfizer. I saw the desperation in their eyes as they suffered a great deal of stress and anxiety about being in a state of limbo, where they straddled the world of the paycheck and longed for the world where work may be more meaningful or secure. "I just need a couple more years until I retire. I'm going to wait for that." one of my colleagues told me.

Other colleagues in the company who were the same age as me were afraid to venture outside for similar reasons of lack of security. They justified staying when they weren't growing for a lot of the same reasons: fear, being comfortable where they were, or hope that they would eventually grow inside.

Luck byte

Hope is important but not a growth strategy.

Then something happened that changed my perspective completely. My boss and good friend of fifteen years died suddenly. He was diagnosed with bladder cancer and in the three months that followed, progressed rapidly downward towards his death. He was sixty-two and was just two to three years away from retirement and getting his full financial benefits when he wouldn't have to work anymore.

He too had spent most of his career at Pfizer and was "waiting for retirement". What a shame, I thought. Years of hard work and devotion only to be stricken with an illness and never making it to retirement.

His sudden passing made me realise that waiting for something good to happen, in his case retirement was a path that I was walking on without realizing such. It was an easy path. The path of least resistance. A path by default of making no change. A path that required no effort and more importantly no active will or choice.

On the easy path, you don't have to do anything different. You don't have to go out of your comfort zone. It doesn't require much work. You wait it out and hope you don't get thrown out. But leaving the company to start a new career, regardless of what I would be giving up, was indeed the hard path.

My friend and boss's sudden death made me realize a truth that is, there is, in fact, no such thing as the easy path. There is only the hard path. You either take that hard path by choice now or you will likely be forced to take it later in life when you have no choice.

Staying in a job and waiting for luck to happen to you seems easy. But as you wait for it to make a guest appearance, opportunities pass by along with the most important asset human beings have: time.

Over time hard paths become easier and easy paths become hard.

I came to the conclusion that in order for me to bring more luck and prosperity and growth into my life, I had to make a choice to leave my job at this great company to pursue a different path. A much harder path. I had to disrupt myself because that's the only way to continue growing. Because I wanted to be a part of this great big shift going on in the world today where technology is reshaping everything. But I would have to give up the financial security that my present job offered. In order for me to experience the shift myself and be part of that new story going on in the world and to grow deeper now and not wait for it, I would have to travel a difficult and uncertain path.

So, I did. I left Pfizer to walk on the hard path.

When you make that decision, that choice to walk on the hard path, two things happen: first—the world doesn't fall apart. No big sirens go off. You don't immediately start suffering and losing money and falling off a cliff. It's not as scary as your mind had assumed it was going to be. Second—life presents you with interesting opportunities. Out of nowhere, you start running into people. Friends you hadn't seen in a while call you out of nowhere.

As I left my corporate career, through a meeting I randomly accepted from a friend, I met the CEO of a small startup company that was working on trying to bring a big idea into the marketplace. They had developed a way to manufacture DNA and insert it into the supply chain and use it as a barcode. Very interesting and exciting technology. It was a small company of fifty people based out of Stony Brook, NY.

The CEO was looking for someone who had experience in the pharmaceutical world to help them bring this big and grand idea into the marketplace. And he asked me to join to help them grow. They didn't have much money to pay me. They didn't have funds—it had to come from fundraising as is typical with most startups. I wouldn't have any resources such as a team of people or investment to make in sales or marketing. And it was a totally new field with lots of hurdles and regulations. It was an unproven technology and looked like a big challenge.

At the same time, I had run into another CEO one of a bigger more established company of fifty years. We had known each other for some years. I began discussions with him about joining his company—a bigger company. Lots of people, more resources, better pay, and benefits.

After leaving Pfizer, I could not have imagined that I would be facing another choice so soon. One choice was the small company with its cool technology but no financial guarantees. The other choice was a bigger company with a tested business model and running a business generating billions of dollars in revenue. The big company was not going out of business anytime soon, whereas there was always a risk at the small company.

After gaining valuable advice from speaking with mentors and friends, I decided to take the hard path again and join the small company that was doing cutting edge work in technology and innovation. I agreed to head business development here.

Since leaving Pfizer and walking on the hard path, I have faced many challenges and obstacles, all of which have forced me to become better, stronger, and sharper in ways I could not have imagined.

Going from a big company with big budgets, a large team and support to a small company with fifty people was a big change. I had to become a student again as I learned about new industries, met new people, and had to deal with difficult situations and circumstances. I faced lots of rejection because I was pitching a new technology in a competitive market. I wasn't used to rejection in my senior role at Pfizer.

Those challenges, obstacles and problems that I faced on the hard path forced me to get out of my comfort zone, think differently, face up to my fears, be creative, develop new ways of looking at things, and become more creative and resourceful.

Through the hard path, I was able to succeed at getting the company into the market place with their new technology. I did it. I was successful not only in achieving the goals set by the company but realised success in doing something not many people get a chance to do: bring a big idea into the marketplace.

Gaining new skills, become stronger mentally, and being able to help the startup achieve success also created a moat around my resume.

Before taking the hard path, I was one of the thousands who "worked at Pfizer", even though I had a remarkable track record of success in the company. I was still one of the many who worked there. I now have the credibility of helping a startup become successful. Of bringing a big idea into the marketplace. By choosing the hard path, I have been able to create a moat around my resume, differentiating me as I move forward towards a new career.

Don't get me wrong here. I don't think that you need to leave your job like I did. What I am saying here is that if you have a deep down desire to grow and experience luck and success, your chances increase when you proactively make choices which are hard. It is because the obstacles and challenges you will face on the hard path force you to dig down deep within yourself to solve problems building the mind muscle and capabilities that improve the way you think, what you know and how you act.

Fear of failure kept me from taking the bold step of leaving my job. Fear of not making it. Fear is a powerful force.

We avoid taking the hard path because this fear outweighs our desire to grow. And so, we avoid doing what is hard. But what I learned was that the same fear of failure can also make you pivot and fuel your journey out of your comfort zone. After leaving my corporate career, it was this fear that made me feel alive for the first time in many years. It is the fear that helps light a fire to reignite the hidden strength we all have inside. A hidden power that aids in lighting up our mind to come up with ideas and opportunities. And that can often be at the core of what helps to propel our luck and success in our lives.

"Doing what is hard is the only path to growth."
-Bob Miglani

Key Learnings

1. We make small decisions that alter the course of our destiny each day. By nature, we often choose the path of least resistance, where there is less work to do and what we think will be a faster return on our investment. We choose the easy path. We believe that if you want to rapidly accelerate your chance of success, you must choose the hard path.

2. Do what is hard. Do what seems impossible. Do what scares you and makes you uncomfortable. Do what is a lot more work. Do what will test your inner strength and challenge your resources. Force yourself to delay gratification. Because no big success was ever achieved overnight. It takes time and patience.

3. You know it's the hard path because it requires a crazy amount of work that scares you. You know it's the hard path when you don't see the outcome of your effort for a long period of time. You know it is the hard path when you feel uncomfortable.

4. Choosing the more difficult path and getting out of your comfort zone helps to create a moat around your business and resume and increases your skills and experience in a way that helps accelerate your progress. Creating a moat means that you are less likely to face competition in your startup or your career. Other people will have a hard time copying you or beating you. You learn more, grow more and put yourself in the space where luck will blossom. This is because the hard path will be full of challenges, obstacles, and problems. And learning how to face those problems will grow your skills, your resiliency, and your success.

Practical tip: The difficult path defined: Marketing campaigns that require more work but less money and give you returns in the longer term; having uncomfortable conversations with those around you that are necessary; not avoiding tough decisions for later; taking action now.

My Action Plan

1. **What is the one big, difficult action that you have been avoiding that you commit to taking now— immediately? What is the hard path that you dedicate yourself to taking?**

....
....
....
....

2. **What could be the positive result of you taking the hard path?**

....
....
....
....

3. **What one hard and difficult conversation do you commit to having today and with whom?**

....
....
....
....

> "You can adapt to anything.
> You just don't know it yet."
> -Bob Miglani

CHAPTER 6

PRACTICE RANDOMNESS

> **"You can't connect the dots looking forward; you can only connect them looking backwards."**
> **-Steve Jobs**

Life is not linear. And neither is success. It does not follow the rules of logic, order, and reason. That's why some of the most unlikely people get lucky in finding an incredible job, marrying an amazing person, or hitting it big with their startup venture.

Discovering success is a messy process. And most often success and luck come from the most unexpected places, from people and opportunities you least expect or imagine.

There is no structured path to achieving great success. Getting from where you are today to where you want to be in the future will not be achieved by walking in a straight line.

If you are hoping to get recognised and be promoted to a better office and a better salary, working hard in your job just doesn't work anymore. There's too much competition and uncertainty in the workplace these days. Funding, hiring, and pitching for your startup using traditional methods are also becoming overused.

There is no well-defined path. Therefore, you have to force yourself to practice randomness. To be open-minded about everything. To think differently and take actions in the most unlikely ways, in the most unlikely places, so that you increase your probability of success.

Since luck and success come from the oddest places and from people who you don't know today and have no idea that you'll meet, you have to cast a wider net to cover a bigger area of people and places.

Does this mean that I pursue everything, all the time?

No. It is not about going around aimlessly without any focus. Practicing randomness is about being open to people and occurrences that you encounter and recognising that there may be something important there. It is about spotting the limits of our ideas and resisting the temptation to close off on anything we don't know or understand.

Here's how:

- **Say yes more than you say no.**

Rehan: If I had not said YES to my friend who had requested me to join one of the early meetings of the Indian Angel Network (angel investing was a concept I had not heard of earlier), I would not have been at the right place at the right time, which was getting on board the angel investing wave that started in India in 2008. Because of this, I invested in amazing entrepreneurs like Bhavish Aggarwal of Ola, Shirish Deodhar of Sapience and many others. Which in turn led to establishing one of India's earliest domestic venture capital funds in 2013, changing my career from an e-commerce entrepreneur to a fund manager and making me part of the very exciting financial services industry in India. At the fund, we invested in more amazing companies like PharmEasy, GoMechanic, Country Delight, and many more.

- **Talk to everyone about your idea, your passion, your interest, the challenges you are facing, or the problem you are trying to solve.**

Bob: Sitting next to someone at dinner in a restaurant in Switzerland, I happened to mention I had been working on my first attempt at writing a book. This man, a consultant, was someone I had met only two or three times and he was part of a larger group of colleagues and consultants working on the same project I was working on for Pfizer. I had never written a book before and had no idea of how to get it published. At a casual conversation over dinner, he initially asked what I did for fun on the weekends. "Well, I'm really passionate about this idea of a book on the lessons I learned running my family's Dairy Queen store," I shared enthusiastically.

After being rejected by fifty or so literary agents to represent my book to publishers, I expressed my problem to this man over our dinner. He smiled and said, "Wow, that's so interesting. You know, my wife is a bestselling author and has one of the top literary agents in the world representing her. I would be happy to introduce you." Amazing! In a random conversation where I shared my need to find a literary agent who could get my book published—this man had a direct connection in the publishing world! Was it kismet? Was it chance? Was it randomness? Yes, it was all those things.

Well, it turned out that he knew a number of people in the publishing world and introduced me to all of them. One of them loved my idea of the book I was writing and agreed to represent me and became my literary agent. And she did a great job at presenting my idea to publishers. Within six months of meeting that man over dinner in Switzerland, I was back in NYC and had signed my first book deal with a major publisher! I was on my way to becoming a real author. A published author by a major publishing company! It was all because I was proactive and shared my passion with a stranger over dinner.

- **Proactively reach out to people whom you would not normally speak to.**

Rehan: As I mentioned in Chapter 2, I met Jaspreet Singh by practicing randomness (though I did not think of it as such at that time), as I proactively reached out to him on a tech forum. My email to him led me to discover an opportunity which eventually led me to invest and realise a massive return of millions on my investment. If both Jaspreet and I didn't have an open mind, who knows if Druva would have ever been born and become the biggest software company to ever come out of India.

- **Don't allow the mind to tell you that it won't work.**

How do you know it won't work? Can you predict the future? Don't try to predict the outcome. Because the mind thinks logically and you have to force it to be more open.

- **Make it a conscious effort of trying non-traditional approaches.**

In an elevator, look at someone in the eye while putting out your hand saying, "Hello. I thought I would introduce myself".

Ask for advice on your idea from someone in a completely different industry and background than you.

Go to a conference or meeting that you would normally never attend.

Accepting Randomness – Rehan

After moving from stagnation in the floral seed import business to online floral delivery, I thought Flora2000 was going to be the one to capture the Indian market. I had a good plan, great website, had built up the massive infrastructure in launching an awesome experience for Indian customers to buy and send flowers online. And then, nothing happened. I launched and waited. Waited and waited. I had got everything right, except for one thing: in 2004 there was hardly anyone online in India.

And then out of nowhere came a random occurrence. We received an order from a US customer who was an Indian living in the US who wanted to send flowers to someone in India. It was one, then a couple more. But again, three or so orders don't make you a business. And it was not the hundreds of orders I was hoping for from Indian consumers.

At that moment, I could have dismissed these three orders as a random occurrence and moved on to spend time focusing on the Indian market. But my curiosity led me to look into this further. I accepted randomness. I didn't dismiss it. I noticed a signal in the marketplace. That's really the key. To be observant of the random nature of our world and to recognise it as a whisper to help shape our direction.

How often do we dismiss random occurrences because they don't fit so neatly into our way of thinking? How many times have we played down or rationalised a chance event because it doesn't make logical sense? How often do we not look into things deeper because it's not how we think the world works?

By looking into the random occurrence of a few orders from the US, I unknowingly dug deep to make sense of the orders to understand why this was happening. When I started digging deeper, my eyes lit up realising that this might be a significant opportunity for my floral business. Not the opportunity I was hoping for or betting on or planning for. It was something different. Maybe better. Maybe worse. I didn't know. But I had to pursue it. I had to see if I could get more orders out of the US for customers who wanted to send flowers to India.

Looking back, it made sense to follow up on that random occurrence but when you're a founder of a startup focused on one mission of your company, it's easy to dismiss random events because you're so busy running a business. You miss small signals that are so important. You're so preoccupied with trying to find more customers, raise money, run marketing, fix the code on the site, and so on. In all the business of starting and running a new company, you lose sight of signs the marketplace is sending you. Signs that often appear random but provide rich bread crumbs that you need to follow. Bread crumbs that lead to the pot of gold hidden beneath seemingly innocent observations.

As a result of digging deeper into those three orders, I discovered that I had to change my whole business. The India orders were not coming in but the US orders could have something here. Everyone in the US paid by credit cards anyway, so could be a more willing audience to buy flowers online for someone in India. Was it big enough?

Was there money to be made here? I didn't know but thought I would give it a shot.

And so, I shifted my business of Flora2000 to focus solely on being a website that allowed people from the US to send flowers to India and eventually to all parts of the world. It wasn't the model that I had planned for but became the model where I found my luck. And it was all because I accepted that random occurrence.

If I wasn't successful in Flora2000, I would not have become an angel investor in Ola, Druva, many others like Sapience, Box8, FabAlley, Unbxd, Jigsee and then Orios, the venture capital fund. Had I not had the foundational learning and eventual cash flow that came from failing and learning and growing Flora2000, I would not have been lucky enough to have such massively successful valuations of my investments.

But how to do this? How to practice randomness in daily life? Does this mean that you chase every little thing?

One way to think about practicing randomness is to think about the places and people and events you are more UNLIKELY to explore. This is because we need to move away from our own biases to a mindset of allowing the market to tell us what we should be doing to serve them. And we can only do that when we proactively seek out unlikely people to pitch or areas of interest to go after.

Rather than thinking about what we think the market needs, we should allow the market to tell us what they need. The customer is the best and only judge of your idea.

You accomplish this by focusing on people, places and

events that you are unlikely to be around or consider. Here's how:

- Expand the diversity of the pool of people you deal with. Networking gurus will tell you the more *diverse* (not just large) your network, the more powerful it is.
- Say yes more often to speaking with people or going to places, which seem unrelated to what you're working on.
- Talk to everyone about your idea, your passion, your interest, the challenges you are facing, or the problem you are trying to solve.
- Always talk to people you sit next to on a plane, a train, a bus, or at dinner.
- Over-share your thoughts (don't be secretive) with random people because you never know what idea they can give you or people they can introduce you to, which can drastically increase the luck you experience.
- Don't allow the mind to tell you that it won't work. How do you know it won't work? Can you predict the future? Don't try to predict the outcome.
- Make a conscious effort of trying non-traditional approaches and reaching out to random people.

Practicing Randomness – Bob

As I became successful as a sales rep in Pfizer, I looked forward to getting promoted and moving up the corporate ladder. I figured that since Pfizer was such a big company with a strong and sophisticated HR process, my manager would come forward to help me find jobs and opportunities. When I gently inquired with him, he told me to be patient and assured me that he would certainly help me find a suitable promotion should one become available. The years of hard work and effort were beginning to pay off as my sales performance was higher each year. I was on track to become the #1 sales rep in my district, among the top ten in the East Coast region, and one of the top in the country. But my manager did not revert on the promotion or job advancement opportunities in the company.

In frustration, I called one of my old college professors who was a wonderful human being and mentor. I reached out to him occasionally to seek advice and vent career frustrations. Over our conversation, he mentioned that I should try to seek out advice from a friend of his, a professor of international business in the PhD program at Pace University located in New York City, which incidentally was part of my sales territory.

Initially, I didn't pay too much attention to his suggestion. "What's the point?" I thought. "How can he possibly help me move up the corporate ladder?" And so, I sat on this connection for a few weeks. Then one day, as I passed the university on my way to make sales calls, I recalled the conversation I had with my college mentor.

As an act of randomness, I decided to call the professor and meet with him. He was kind enough to invite me to lunch where we talked about what I was doing and the kinds of programs he was running for his doctoral students. I mentioned that I was interested in international business, the subject he was teaching and offered to help him with projects. He liked my enthusiasm for volunteering and mentioned that he needed help in getting speakers for one of his classes. He liked to bring in outside speakers for his international business PhD class and asked me if I knew anyone at Pfizer headquarters who might be interested in speaking to the class. I couldn't think of anyone right away but promised to think about it.

As I got home that evening, an idea occurred to me. Why not reach out to someone at Pfizer Inc. corporate headquarters and ask them to speak at this professor's class? It might be a good way for me to get to know someone in corporate headquarters and at the same time, help the professor.

Being in the field force, I didn't have access to the corporate directory in those days. So, I found whatever I could in the public domain and got the name of the #2 person at Pfizer Inc. His name was Robert Neimeth and he was the President of Pfizer International. Initially, my own doubts held me back. His position was way too high for him to pay attention to a request to speak from someone so low on the corporate ladder. Or so I assumed. I finally wrote a simple letter to him, requesting him to speak at the professor's class.

Following up on that letter, I called the Pfizer corporate office and was connected to his secretary. I asked her if Mr Neimeth would be willing to talk at Pace University. She said that he enjoyed doing these things for students and would indeed be willing to do it. This was huge news for me. I had succeeded in getting the President of Pfizer International, the #2 person in the company, to agree to speak at the professor's class.

The professor was pleased to hear the news and arranged a date in the coming months. At this time, I was twenty-six years old and had no idea what I was doing. Had no idea of how to handle such a thing with someone of such high stature in the company. So, I called his secretary again and said that I had arranged a date and that on the day of the speaking event, I would pick him up and drive him downtown to Pace University to deliver his presentation. She agreed and noted the date and told me that Mr Neimeth, being a corporate officer of the company had a car with a driver who would take him to the event. As soon as she said that my hopes of getting to know this man start diminishing. I did some quick thinking and asked her, "Well, in that case, would you mind if I drove down with him in his car?" I asked such a naive question and received the perfect answer: "Sure, why not, Bob. I'm sure Mr Neimeth would enjoy your company."

The date of the speaking event arrived and I drove up to Pfizer's corporate office and met the man himself. At 6'3" Pfizer's President, International division, was a tall man with a boyish face wearing round glasses as he had just come from a meeting. We shook hands and then, drove to downtown NYC towards Pace University. During the ride, I remember his curiosity, asking me a number of questions as to what I was doing at Pfizer, what was going on with customers, our products, our competitors, and much more. The ride lasted twenty minutes before we reached our destination. He proceeded to give his talk to the PhD class, which went very well. Later, as we said goodbye, I thanked him for his time and proceeded to ask one final question. "Mr Neimeth, would you mind if I call you for advice sometime?" What I actually wanted to say was that I was interested in getting into the international division, but hesitated. He said, "Yes, of course, Bob. Call me anytime. Happy to speak to you."

He left, driving back to midtown NYC to the corporate office where I wished I worked. After years of success in sales, that's where I wanted to be and now, I had met someone who might possibly help me get there.

The next day, I called his secretary to thank her for her help in coordinating Mr Neimeth's talk. I also practiced randomness by mentioning to her that I would be contacting Mr Neimeth in six months for advice when I finished the part-time MBA program that I was studying for in the evenings. I explained that I had this crazy dream of working in the international division of Pfizer. Since I had gotten to know her a little bit over our few phone calls, she asked, "Bob, when you met him, did you tell him of your interest?" "No, I didn't mention it specifically", I answered.

Then she told me the obvious but with simple clarity, "If you want something, you have to ask for it. If you want his advice, don't wait. Ask him now. Why wait six months? Write to him, showing your interest with your resume and I will make sure he reads it." I felt kind of silly for not telling him when I met him. I guess I was scared of asking directly because he was such a senior person. And so, thanks to his secretary, I gained the confidence to reach out to him.

Only two weeks later, after I sent my letter of thanks along with my resume to Mr Neimeth, I received a phone call from the head of human resources at Pfizer. "My boss seems impressed with you and he wants me to meet you right away," said the head of Human Resources on the phone. Shocked and a bit nervous but hopeful at the same time, I said yes, "I'm happy to meet you."

After spending about two hours with the Head of Human Resources at Pfizer, I was offered the opportunity for a job interview with the head of the International Pricing Department. When I read the job description, I was anxious because I didn't have any of the qualifications listed. I didn't have an MBA in Finance, Accounting, or Information Management experience. As I walked away after the interview, I spotted Mr Neimeth heading to his office on the same floor. I followed him and poked my head into his office to say hello. I mentioned that I had just met with the head of HR who suggested I interview for the job in the Pricing Department. "Yes, Pricing is one of the most strategic areas for the company. It's a good role and you'd be ideal for it," he said.

"But I don't have any pricing experience, Mr Neimeth," I blurted. "Don't worry, you'll learn all that. What's really important is that you know the customers, the products, and the competitors and that's really the heart of the business. Go for it," he said, encouragingly.

With his backing, I felt a little more confident and accepted the job interview. The interviews went well and the head of the department, a Scottish Chartered Accountant named Ian Young was thrilled at having me join them and offered me the job right away.

I looked at the paper with the job offer along with the requirements for the job. It was surreal. I was being offered double my salary to work in a function where I had no experience. Boy, was I lucky, I thought at the time. I get to work in the international division of Pfizer where I always dreamed of working. Making more money and not even having finished my MBA program.

Was it random? Was it luck? Was it chance? Was it work? Yes, to all of those things. I had to work hard at becoming a #1 sales rep so that helped boost my resume. But what got me from point A to point B—from being one of thousands in the field of sales reps to a department of four in a corporate headquarters job was Practicing Randomness. It wasn't linear. It wasn't through the process of waiting for my boss to find me opportunities. It was owning my life, owning my own opportunities, and owning the idea of practicing randomness that helped me succeed in achieving growth in my career.

Key Learnings

1. Success is not linear and orderly. It is messy, unstructured, and unpredictable. Success is often found in places and from people who are unlikely to be in your current circle of friends, colleagues, or loved ones.

2. So, what do we do if success is unpredictable? Do unpredictable things. You have to increase your odds with proactive attempts to reach those people and places where you will discover success. You must practice randomness so that you increase your odds of reaching the right person at the right time. Force yourself to reach beyond the scope of your comfort zone.

3. Become passionate about your cause, purpose, or goals. Create a sense of enthusiasm and wonder. Talk to

strangers about your ideas and passion. Pitch the bus driver. Share your story with others. Ask to help others. Go out and meet people you normally would not meet. Join groups or associations that you normally would not join.

My Action Plan

1. **What are the uncommon actions I plan to take?**

   ....
   ....
   ....
   ....

2. **I make a commitment to speaking to unusual and random people that I will reach out to or come across about my ideas, my passion, my interests and my business. Sign your name below:**

   ....

3. **I commit to saying YES to invitations to meet new people, go to new events or opportunities where I would not normally go.**

   ....
   ....
   ....
   ....

   "Always give randomness a
   chance to surprise you."
   -Bob Miglani

CHAPTER 7

HAVE MULTIPLE PLAN 'A'S. ALWAYS BE EXPERIMENTING (ABE)

"Everyone has a plan until they get punched in the mouth."
-Mike Tyson, Heavyweight
Boxing Champion

Many people obsess over finding success by discovering "The One".

The one idea that's going to make it big.

The one business that will set up the course of our lives.

The one job.

The one company.

The one career.

The one marketing strategy.

The one big promotion.

The one perfect plan.

We want "The One" to solve all of our problems and to give us the financial success that will help us get totally set for life.

Yes, ideally it is wonderful to have that one plan that can guarantee huge success.

What we have learned however is that there is no such thing as "The One". And there are no guarantees in life.

There is no one idea.

There is no one job.

There is no one plan.

The phrase in the business world that says, "Go big or go home" just doesn't work.

It suggests that if we're going to make it as a business or as a professional in pursuit of greatness, we must back this one idea, this one goal, this one concept. We must back it with all our might and with all our investment, with all of our strength and resources. And if we succeed, it will be amazing. It will be a huge win when we succeed.

This concept is great if you are 100% sure that the one idea you have is going to be accepted by your customers, your boss, or the marketplace. Otherwise, it is flawed and can lead to disaster in your business, your career, or your life.

And that is because we can never ever be sure which path or plan, which product, or which strategy will work. The marketplace changes too fast.

No one really knows what's going to work and what's not.

No path is 100% guaranteed to be sure.

And so, before you focus and put all your efforts behind one particular strategy or other, you have to experiment. A lot. And continue experimenting. Doing so will lead to lots of failures. And in that process, also discovering success. You will increase your odds of being lucky. Of finding the one or two things that really work well which will become the foundation of your luck and of your success moving forward.

And therefore, instead of just backing Plan A, one idea, one product, one approach and backing it big time, we believe it is better to have Multiple Plan 'A's. Until you have found that one thing that works so well, you have to do a lot of experimentation.

We believe that you will dramatically increase your odds of success by trying multiple Plan 'A's, at the **same time**.

Not one Plan A. And if that doesn't work, trying Plan B and then Plan C and so on. A sequential Plan A, Plan B, Plan C, and so on takes too long.

Instead, the key is trying two or three things with limited budgets at the **same time** and letting the marketplace be the best judge of what will work and what will not.

Always be experimenting in your business and in your life. Make small bets on initiatives, projects, and ideas and implement them simultaneously. This does two things: reduces risk of total failure and increases your odds of success in a shorter span of time.

Conventional Mindset	**Luck Mindset**
Go with "The One"	Try multiple Plan 'A's
Bet a lot on one	Bet a little on each
Wait and see; Go to Plan B	Do it all at the same time

No one can predict the future. No one can predict which career path will be better in the end. No one can predict which idea, product, or service will be a hit with the customer. No one can predict if your startup will make it—not the best venture capitalist, not your parents, not your friends, and not you.

There are just too many variables to make accurate predictions. Especially these days with so much competition.

Only the marketplace is the true judge of what's going to work and what's going to fail. So, you have to try. And keep trying. Even when you have a great business—because the customer changes all the time.

The problem most people have in the quest for success is that they bet too heavily on what they assume will work. And they bet all their resources on that one thing. The reality is you never know what will really work and what won't.

The marketplace doesn't necessarily respond to what you think they will respond to. Customers are unpredictable. The marketplace changes too fast.

And if you bet too heavily on one Plan A, it often can drain all your resources leaving you with nothing to bounce back on. This is because the risk of failure with one plan is so high with no resources left to recover.

According to the article *Finding Your Company's Second Act* published in the Harvard Business Review in January 2018,

*". . . companies fail when they focus all
their resources into a single product . . ."*

Quoting from the article:

*"In studying companies that faced second-act crises, we found
that the leading cause of premature death was, ironically,
that their executives had enthusiastically embraced the latest
management ideas. In the name of concepts such as "design
thinking," "lean," and "agile" development, they focused
resources and creativity on making first-generation products
as compelling as possible—on delivering a superior if not
"delightful" customer experience for each user. But in the
process, they ended up limiting the assets of the organization
to those necessary to complete a single mission.*

*To be sure, even in the era of big-bang disruption, managers
need to stay focused on business fundamentals, including
careful management of fixed costs, capital assets, product
inventory, and human resources. But an inflexible obsession
with a single product or a single customer segment leads more
often than not to a second-act crisis."*

Don't Believe Conventional Wisdom – Rehan

I was an entrepreneur who had found success serving a
deep and narrow niche in the online floral delivery market.

As I continued to grow, the conventional thinking was to reinvest the profits from Flora2000 back into the business. I had done this for a while but realised that here was the risk of too much concentration. Who knew when my luck would run out? Maybe the closure in the telecom and floral seed import business made me a little nervous because both businesses were doing well and then had to be exited. I was a little worried about having all my eggs in one basket. And so, I started thinking about other things I could do but wasn't really sure exactly what they would be. Listening to what others were doing, I tried my hand at investing in real estate and lost some money. I realised that I was neither interested in those traditional approaches nor good at it.

But soon I was introduced to Angel Investing. I started investing in startups like Ola Cabs, Druva, Faballey, Unbxd, Box8 and many others. I knew how to run a successful startup and so I knew that I could help them grow. As I continued my angel investing, I began to realise that I really enjoyed helping startup founders and companies navigate their journey. And shortly after, I made the decision to step back from the day-to-day management of my own startup Flora2000. If I was going to do this full-time, I couldn't just do it as an angel investor. In order to really help the startups make it big, I had to create and launch a venture capital fund and do it on a large scale. So, I decided to launch one of India's earliest domestic VC funds of Rs.300 crores ($50 million) in 2013.

Conventional Thinking to Forward Thinking

I knew how to invest but that was only a part of the business. I knew how to run a startup and be an angel investor, but didn't know how to be a venture capitalist. I certainly didn't know how to get people to give me millions of dollars for a venture capital fund.

As I began investing in startups in India as an angel in 2008, I was doing it mostly with my own money that I had saved over the years from running Flora2000. But running a VC fund is very different. You have to go out and raise funds from investors who were going to trust you with their money. When I started asking people who were running the handful of VC funds in India, they would tell me that India wasn't ready for VC funds and advised me not to waste my time going after investors in India. "Go west. Go to the US" was the advice I received. America had a more developed venture capital market and more money to invest. And there was the possibility of investors from places in Asia such as Singapore, where there was more money to invest in new and emerging technologies.

Sitting on this idea I had for starting $50 million fund was a daunting task. I had put in most of my savings into the fund and I needed to find a way to make it work. Everyone was telling me to go to the US and I was starting to believe them. But as I started packing my bags to head there, I had this thought: How do they know? How can they be so sure? That model probably worked in the past. How do they know what the future holds? Just because something worked in the past was no guarantee that it was going to work now.

They couldn't be so sure. Neither could I.

I wasn't convinced of the hypothesis of either past experiences or the experts.

So, I decided to implement Multiple Plan 'A's to raise $50 million for my first venture capital fund. Instead of simply doing what everyone else did, which was to go to US institutions to ask them to invest in a VC fund in India, I decided to go three places: the US, parts of Asia, specifically Singapore, and go where no one was ever successful—India.

I had a very limited budget as none of my angel investments were cashed out and had to use my limited financial resources in several places.

I approached my fundraising in the US, India, and Singapore as small experiments. Most of my work involved heavy travel including twenty-hour flights, staying in hotels in busy, crowded cities, and spending days on the road as the budget was mostly for travel. I flew economy class, stayed in small, cheap hotels on the outskirts of major cities, and took the cheapest transportation everywhere. I spread my limited budget over many places instead of concentrating only on the US, as most fundraisers traditionally had done.

At times I thought what I was doing was crazy. Especially as I was sitting in multiple airports in a single week. I was exhausted from travelling, driving, being on buses, trains. Sleeping in lumpy beds in cheap hotels in the rain, snow, and heat. The doubts crept in during those moments of tiredness. Maybe I should really focus on one thing. Isn't that the way I should do it? Safer? But I resisted the temptation to cut off my plans **until the marketplace told me what was right and what was wrong**. I didn't want my opinion or the opinion of others to dictate what my customers should be telling me.

As it turned out, the US was not the place I was going to find investors for my first fund. It was closer to home— it was India. Indian investors had never been approached before and many said "no". But many said "yes". Some believed in the hope—the promise of homegrown startups that could succeed in this new economy. And many believed in the vision I was putting forward of a homegrown startup ecosystem to launch India's great companies of the future.

In the end, I was able to raise my $50 million fund entirely from India.

The marketplace voted. The verdict came not from the voices and opinions of others or me—the verdict came from the investors themselves.

That's the true source of success, of luck—listening to customers. Letting the customers tell you which plan is right and which plan is wrong.

After my first fund closed, I was able to use a very similar strategy to raise my second fund. And today, I use this same philosophy in managing where I deploy the fund, as I do with strategies I suggest to the companies where we invest.

Ola Cabs is constantly experimenting. They launched Ola bikes, Ola Buses, Ola Select, Ola Australia, Ola UK and many more. Some flopped but some did very well. They learned and then invested more in the things that worked.

Google constantly experiments. The first was to move themselves out of only the search business. They created Alphabet, the parent company of Google. So that they could place more "bets" on other projects. Google Fiber. Google Space. Waymo. Some are failing but some such as Waymo hold a lot of promise.

The idea of only sticking to one core competency for a company has been completely destroyed by Jeff Bezos, founder of Amazon. Amazon is in multiple businesses that have little to do with one other. Amazon has gone beyond experimentation as an exercise and this seems to be embedded in the very DNA of everything they do. They are relentless in experimenting. Amazon Prime Video to Alexa to Cloud services to books and apparel. And they do this simultaneously, not sequentially. That's the key to try many things at the same time.

> **"This will not go the way you think."**
> **-Luke Skywalker**

Life Is A Series of Experiments – Bob

Around the time of the world financial crisis in 2008, I felt everything changed. Every business, every company, every career, including my own, was under threat. I was fearful of losing my job at Pfizer thanks to the cuts the company was making in all divisions. Even though I was a successful executive who had been there a long time with mentors and leaders who valued my work, I felt worried and anxious about an uncertain future. The world was changing, how could I not realise that the certainty of a long career in one company was coming to an end? My boss was nervous too because he was being asked to cut budgets in his department including reducing headcount. Even though he was senior and had excellent relationships, the changes to the company's business environment forced everyone to rethink their plans.

If my department was cut, then I would be forced to find a job in another department at Pfizer, where there was no certainty or security.

Sixteen years in a big company having experienced so much success and enjoyment, I suddenly found myself being stuck between the past idea of what was once certainty and security of a long career in one company to the great big unknown. With so much change, the future that I once used to see with hope looked bleaker as the financial crisis deepened.

As I started to come out of the mental state of fear and worry, I realised that I needed to try something new with my career. But I wasn't sure what to do. I liked working at Pfizer but the world outside of technology and emerging biotechnology was growing rapidly. Whole new economies were being shaped. I did realise one thing for sure and that was: **no one knows how the future is going to turn out.** No one knows which strategy will work. No one knows what the right path is going to be moving forward. No one.

Several people in the company who were big shots—who I thought would have job security forever—were let go during the massive organisational change in the company and found themselves out of a job.

I realised in those months that I needed to change my

thinking. I had to change my strategy. Of how I looked at my career and my life.

Plan A in My Job

And so, I began to try something new to reinvigorate my career at Pfizer. My plan was to do something no one else had done—something valuable for my department and the company. Since I was in the medical partnerships role, I set a bold goal for myself to bring in a big partner to the company. By bringing in a new partner, I thought it would help prove my value.

Over the course of several months, I reached out to many people in my network and started a series of discussions and brainstorming ideas. One friend referred me to a friend of his named Steve Cone at a big organisation called AARP, who was working on projects in healthcare and caregiving. Even though this organisation wasn't a medical one, it was doing something interesting and important around healthcare. Steve and I started brainstorming together and over the course of a year started to build out a partnership between AARP and Pfizer, which was eventually launched after a year.

After almost two years of experimenting with multiple Plan 'A's, I found success. This was a huge development in my career because so many others had tried to build this partnership over the years with AARP. However, I was able to finally implement it successfully. My experiment had paid off and helped not only secure my job but also grow my career and standing in the company by bringing a valuable partner to the company. Other colleagues whose jobs were threatened weren't so lucky. They didn't do anything different. They didn't experiment. They didn't try anything new. They didn't grow. In fact, some of them lost their jobs due to restructuring. A lot of it had to do with this mindset of understanding that the world changes quickly and we must adapt and change ourselves if we're going to be successful. Some people don't accept that they have to change and so resist adapting and trying anything new.

But I didn't stop there.

Plan A with My Spouse

I realised I also needed a backup plan for my family in case I would not be working for Pfizer. And my wife would be leading that plan. As an eye doctor, she was working part-time while trying to raise our two baby daughters. She had the idea of opening up her own practice but was not really committed until 2008 when we both realised that it might be a good idea for the longer term for her to have her own business. It would be our Plan B (actually our second Plan A). It was a difficult choice because it would mean that I would have to help her on the weekends and give up any free time. So, we signed a lease in a building so she could start her practice in 2009, at the height of the financial crisis. Business loans weren't easy at the time so we had to reach into our savings to start the business.

Although I had grown up around a small family business, neither of us had any experience in running our own medical and healthcare business. But we were committed to trying something new to grow our lives.

My wife worked seven days a week to build her business while I helped as much as I could on the weekends, even acting as her receptionist a few times at the front desk because we didn't have enough resources to hire staff in the beginning. Building a new business from nothing required us to experiment in terms of marketing as well. Since we were new to the business, we didn't go for big dollar expenditures. Instead, we tried small investments in many things such as direct mail, Google AdWords, local community magazine ads, blogging, YouTube, events, seminars, speaking, and other traditional methods.

What we learned was that only two things really worked well in the beginning, which was the local magazine ads and speaking at community events. Even within the local magazine ads, we experimented with different variations, sometimes on the cover of the magazine and other times inside the magazine. And slowly over the course of ten years, the business has grown tremendously. But we haven't stopped experimenting. In fact, as the business grew, so did the number of competitors. And to keep growing, we needed to be ahead of the competition and the only way to do that was to continue experimenting.

The success in my wife's Plan A not only gave us some financial resources for other things but it also gave me valuable skills on marketing—especially online marketing—and this helped me in my other Plan A.

Plan A as a US-India Advisor

Around the same time, as I was trying to reinvent my career at Pfizer and also implement my wife's plan in a new business, I started receiving phone calls from friends about new ideas. As the economy in the US was uncertain, there was a resurgence of interest in doing business in India.

Through a few friends, I was being asked for advice on how to do business in India. As a trusted professional working in Pfizer, I had done business in numerous countries including India, the country of my birth. It turned out that a number of business people both in India and in the US were looking for help from trusted advisors on doing partnerships. One friend, in particular, started inviting me to evening events, weekend lunches, and coffee meetings with entrepreneurs who would ask for my advice on their business projects and deal-making in India.

There were several project proposals seeking my involvement in their deals ranging from energy projects from the US to India, to environmental deals to media initiatives. Since I worked full-time for Pfizer and wasn't really interested, I refused to get involved. Instead, I provided names and contacts of people that might be helpful. I wasn't sure if any of these meetings were going to lead me anywhere but I continued to have these informal conversations because I was committed to say "yes" to a mindset of experimentation. That's how great careers are made, through trial and error. So why not meet?

In one particular experimentation meeting through a friend, I met someone who actually helped change the course of my life. His name is Ben. He was involved in some energy projects and was curious to see if there was a market for his services in India. He asked if I was willing to accompany him to India for a week to explore the scope for business deals in India. I wasn't too keen initially because I didn't see how I could add value. I was also busy working on reinventing my own career and helping my wife launch her business.

But something inside of me said, "just say yes and see what happens, try it." So, I took a vacation from my job for ten days and accompanied him to India on this exploratory trip. On our journey together we met many interesting people—some in business, others in government and also entrepreneurs. During this trip with this new friend, through some funny and chance experiences in meeting people in Ahmedabad, I realised how messy and unpredictable life can be.

When I got back to the US, I shared some funny stories of my trip to India and some of the lessons that I learned that could be applied in our life here in America. One of the people hearing these stories remarked, "Bob, these are great stories about facing uncertainty and moving forward. You really should write a blog and maybe a book about how we can embrace the chaos of life these days in uncertain and changing times. People would benefit from hearing those stories."

This woman happened to be a major force in the publishing world in the US so I took her words seriously. I was astounded and shocked at the profound truth she stated so clearly. People's lives are being turned upside down today because of the uncertainty of life around us in these times of change and uncertainty. And through learning about the messy and often unpredictable way of life in India, they might gain perspective and insight. Through that conversation, I realized that my life journey of learning to deal with disruption and change, I might help others find success in their own journey.

Plan A of Writing a Blog, Then a Book

With the idea of sharing life lessons from India, I began another experiment. Another Plan A. I began writing a simple blog about how to embrace the chaos in life in present times. I had no idea how to write a blog but I learned. I experimented in lots of different ways. The blog became popular, along with a following on Facebook and other platforms. I now found myself on the weekends not in coffee shops meeting people who wanted to do business in India but in the public library where I would be writing a blog post about getting unstuck and moving forward successfully.

Gradually, my writing improved, my audience grew and I was able to get a book deal to publish my life lessons into a book, which was launched in October 2013. It hit the Washington Post bestseller list. From there my speaking career began to take off and I was invited to speak to companies who were going through change and disruption.

In 2016 I left Pfizer to focus on my new career as a bestselling author, speaker, and advisor to companies. I love what I do especially when I have positively impacted someone else's life.

When change and disruption hit my established and structured life, I was forced to try other ways to get to what I believed was success: meaningful work that I was good at, that I would be paid for. And I wasn't sure what that was.

I introduced multiple Plan 'A's not only in my life and career but also in my day job, at the work I was doing.

I didn't implement multiple Plan 'A's because I knew that it was the right approach. I did it because I didn't know. I had no clue which direction I was going to take in my life and neither did anyone else. Trying a little of this and a little of that without spending too much money or risking my day job was the only way I was going to figure it out. Because no one knows what's really going to work and what's not until you try it.

Leaving my job when I didn't know what I was going to do was taking a huge risk. It turns out that I finally did discover what worked. Of all the things I tried, there were three things that worked very well: reinventing my role to bring in the big partner to the company, my wife's optometry business and my book, speaking, and advisory career. And within these things, there were lots of little experiments on marketing, promotion, and trying to reach customers.

One point to note is that once you do figure out what works, then you have to go deep on that one thing because it is physically impossible to do all of those things well at the same time.

In my journey, the most important thing I did was to unknowingly implement multiple Plan 'A's.

I experimented in many ways in my job at Pfizer, in trying new ideas for businesses, in helping my wife open and launch her business and an exploratory trip to India. The trip to India with the friend led me on the path of writing a book and now becoming an advisor to companies, a coach, and a thought leader. I could not have imagined that I would find myself in this role back in 2008 when I first thought of making experimental changes in my life that have led me to much luck, success, and happiness.

Even if you are pursuing one job or business, you should keep on experimenting with different ways to make them better. With the way things are moving so fast, businesses get disrupted and outdated. Jobs and careers change with automation often getting irrelevant. Always be experimenting.

> **"Empty your mind. Be formless,**
> **shapeless, like water."**
> **-Bruce Lee**

Key Learnings

1. Always be experimenting in your life, business, job, career, and strategy. Develop the mindset that you should try many different ways to find the path to success.
2. Instead of betting big on one idea and waiting to see how that will do, place smaller bets with fewer resources on two or three ideas at the same time, which give you data and feedback on what will work and what won't work and then, once you find what works, go deeper.
3. Don't wait for one plan to fail to try another plan. Implement multiple plans at the SAME time. Because

the marketplace moves so fast, you must try things simultaneously and not wait.

My Action Plan

1. **What are the areas of my life where I commit to experimenting? Health, career, job, strategy, relationships, others?**

    ....
    ....
    ....
    ....

2. **What are three experiments I will do in the next 3 months?**

    1. ....
    2. ....
    3. ....

3. **What are the 5 things I always wanted to try in my life and commit to trying right now, today?**

    ....
    ....
    ....
    ....

IN CLOSING

Many have looked up to the heavens and wondered, why not me? Why is someone else getting lucky and not me? Why are they so lucky? Why not me? How come that person is born in the right family? How come their business is doing so well? Why is that person so lucky with their career and not me? Why are their sales growing and not mine? Why is that startup getting funded and not mine?

What we have realised in our journey is that there are a lot of things in life that are not in our control. And too often we get stuck on our path towards success and luck because we get trapped by comparisons—what others have and what we do not. And blame it on luck.

That stops today. Because we want to tilt the balance of luck in your favour.

Yes, we recognise that there are always going to be random and chance occurrences that happen to other people which give them luck and success. That's just life.

But what we have shared with you in this book is an opportunity to get closer to success. We want to turn the odds in your favour. To turn the principles that brought someone else luck to your advantage. To increase your chances.

We believe that luck and success are the result of CHOICES and CHANCES.

Choices that we make.

Chances that we take.

Even though some choices and chances were completely out of our control, we have learned that there are many choices and chances that are indeed under our power.

Unconventional choices that you make every day about the mindset that you have. About the people you surround yourself with. About the goals, you set for your life. About the actions, you take each day. Choices that are under your control. Not the gifts bestowed to you from heaven.

Chances that come upon which you need to pay close attention to. Chances that you need to take which don't at first seem logical. Chances that open you up to the people and places you normally would not take.

Once you refocus your thinking and shift away from luck as something so uncertain to something that can be attracted into your life through living these seven principles, we believe you can increase the odds of luck appearing in your life.

That's indeed what we want, isn't it? A little edge. A tiny advantage. A small breakthrough.

We want you to be wildly successful. We want your startup to succeed. We want your sales career to be the best in the industry. We want your career to take off to the sky. We want you to grow from wherever you are in the company to become whatever you wish to be at the top. We want you to become successful in your life. We want you to achieve the financial success that you dream of.

We also believe that despite today's competitive climate, you can become successful and lucky beyond your wildest dreams. These are extraordinary times we live in where anything is possible with a burning desire, an open mind, and a dedicated heart—practicing these seven principles with commitment and effort.

But to achieve the things you want, you must stop waiting.

Stop waiting for perfect plans to unfold.

Stop waiting for someone to give you a promotion.

Stop waiting for someone to notice your value.

Stop waiting for your startup to get funded.

Stop waiting for customers to buy.

Stop waiting for luck to appear in your life.

Start thinking differently than what so many others have been telling you.

Start taking the unconventional path.

Start making your own luck.

By following our seven unique and unconventional principles of success and luck, we believe you can greatly increase the odds of success in your favour. Whether you're working in sales, trying to launch your startup or climb the corporate ladder, or achieve just about anything in life, embrace these principles fully and commit to them to greatly accelerate your chances of success.

Wishing you all the best of luck in your life.

Bob Miglani   Rehan Yar Khan

LUCKY LISTS

Rehan's 5 Elements of a Good Pitch

1. Start with the problem you saw, wanted to solve, and your solution. Tell a story.
2. Cover market size, competition, and the product's economics.
3. Talk about what the barrier to entry will be.
4. Talk about yours and your co-founders' achievements.
5. Create a business plan in advance and have a definitive ask.

One thing to avoid: Don't spend too much time talking about the product and engineering.

Rehan's 5 Things Every Business Plan Needs to Have

1. Growth projections backed by substance
2. A product that has (or can have) good gross margins

3. Team costs that are always a little below what is desired
4. Low fixed costs
5. Profit in the not-too-distant future!

One thing to avoid: Unrealistic revenue projections. Keep it real to give the confidence that you're sensible.

Bob's Big 5 Sales Accelerators

1. Think like your customer. Your customer doesn't care about you, your idea, your product, or your service. They care about themselves. They care about their problems. They care about their lives. See everything from this perspective. If you can help the customer achieve what they want or need—they will help you achieve super sales success.
2. Prepare, prepare, prepare. Ask and learn everything about your customer. Read. Talk. Listen. Research. Think. Write.
3. Use rejection as an opportunity to get better.
4. Become a great storyteller. Stories move people. Data and facts bore people. Share a story—don't sell a product; tell a story that is relevant, entertaining, and memorable—and ultimately meaningful to the customer.
5. Increase the frequency of rejection—yes—create a rejector's club. Reward yourself for the most rejection.

Rehan's 5 Tips for Hiring for Your Startup

1. Before you start hiring, identify your company's values, so you can check if a candidate has those values.
2. Ensure you have met many candidates and have a shortlist of at least three from which to choose one.
3. Read a good book on interviewing (*Who* by Brad Smart is a great book).
4. The most important quality to look for is proactiveness.
5. Let the candidate ask you questions because you can learn a lot about a person by the questions they ask.

One thing to avoid: Don't miss doing reference checks!

Bob's Big 5 Promotion Accelerators

1. Show up early, all the time and be ready and open-minded to doing good work.
2. Ask really good questions that are deep and thoughtful. Read so you can be ready to ask those questions.
3. Learn from every person you meet. Respect the knowledge and experience from every person you meet.
4. Experiment with new projects. Volunteer. Participate in new initiatives.
5. Do something new, interesting, and valuable that creates value for the company.

ABOUT THE AUTHORS

BOB MIGLANI

Bob moved to the US from India with his family at the age of nine with nothing more than $75 and a desire to pursue the American dream. He mowed lawns, delivered newspapers, and helped his family run their Dairy Queen ice-cream shop in New Jersey.

It was there that he learned the valuable lessons of hard work and a positive can-do attitude, which became the subject of his first book about sales and customer service titled, Treat Your Customers (Hyperion 2006).

Bob started his professional career at the bottom, as a Sales Rep for Pfizer Inc. in Manhattan, one of the most competitive places in the world, where he turned around a sales territory making it #1. For over twenty-three years, he moved up the career ladder creating new functions and opportunities, leading others, and working with customers and colleagues in over thirty countries as an accomplished executive with Pfizer Inc. in NYC.

Bob wrote his second book, *The Washington Post* Bestseller, Embrace the Chaos (Berrett-Koehler 2013) which launched him onto the global stage as a master storyteller, inspiring motivational speaker, advisor to CEOs, and an authority on finding success in times of change and uncertainty. Today Bob works with CEOs, leaders and companies to help them adapt to change and grow by bringing big, new ideas to market.

Bob lives outside New York City.

Reach Bob: @bobmiglani on Twitter, Facebook and YouTube and his blog: www.bobmiglani.com

REHAN YAR KHAN

Rehan is an entrepreneur and venture capital investor. He is well-recognised for his investments in

- OlaCabs, a new-gen taxi aggregator, now India's largest taxi company
- Druva, a world leader in continuous data protection for laptops and servers
- PharmEasy, a pioneer in home-delivering medicine.
- Country Delight, fresh and pure milk and allied products brand
- GoMechanic, which is remaking automobile after service using technology

As an entrepreneur, he built three companies. The first was in 1992, supplying plant materials to farmers across India. The second was a telecom rerouting business. His last venture was Flora2000.com, the first e-commerce company from India for the US consumer market.

In 2008 Rehan began early-stage investing and advising startups in India—initially as an angel and subsequently, as a partner in Orios Venture Partners, a firm he founded.

In the process of building his own companies and experiencing the ups and downs of his entrepreneurial journey, and working with the talented and driven entrepreneurs behind his successful investments, Rehan learnt that failure is a learning opportunity and luck favours the prepared.

He is a passionate advocate of the new wave of entrepreneurship in India through his involvement with The Indian Venture Capital Association (Executive Council) and The Indus Entrepreneurs (TiE). He is involved in the formulation of government policy for the startup ecosystem and efforts behind the holistic development of the space in India.

Rehan lives in Mumbai.